My Name is
STASZEK SURDEL

The Improbable Holocaust Survival of
NATHAN POREMBA
The Last Jew of Wieliczka

JOEL S. POREMBA

Mechanicsburg, PA USA

Published by Sunbury Press, Inc.
Mechanicsburg, Pennsylvania

SUNBURY PRESS

www.sunburypress.com

For information about special discounts for bulk purchases, please contact Sunbury Press Orders Dept. at (855) 338-8359 or orders@sunburypress.com.

To request one of our authors for speaking engagements or book signings, please contact Sunbury Press® Publicity Dept. at publicity@sunburypress.com.

EXPANDED HARDCOVER EDITION: April 2022

Set in Adobe Garamond | Interior design by Crystal Devine | Cover by David Lebovitz | Edited by Lawrence Knorr.

Publisher's Cataloging-in-Publication Data
Names: Poremba, Joel S., author.
Title: My name is Staszek Surdel : the improbable Holocaust survival of Nathan Poremba, the last Jew of Wieliczka / Joel S. Poremba.
Description: Expanded hardcover edition. | Mechanicsburg, PA : Sunbury Press, 2022.
Summary: After the Holocaust, Simon Wiesenthal paraphrased an SS officer who taunted concentration camp prisoners by saying that even if they survived the world would never believe their stories, that the described events would be too monstrous to ever be believed. Nathan Poremba's testimony of Nazi genocide and Polish antisemitism before, during, and after the Holocaust bring credibility to the monstrous events he witnessed and survived.
Identifiers: ISBN 978-1-62006-918-9 (hardcover).
Subjects: HISTORY / Holocaust | HISTORY / Europe / Poland | BIOGRAPHY & AUTOBIOGRAPHY / Survival | BIOGRAPHY & AUTOBIOGRAPHY / Personal Memoirs | BIOGRAPHY & AUTOBIOGRAPHY / Historical.

Product of the United States of America
0 1 1 2 3 5 8 13 21 34 55

Continue the Enlightenment!

CONTENTS

FOREWORD

The Holocaust survivor story of Nathan Poremba acts as a remarkable conduit into the first-hand account of the journey of discovery by a caring and devoted son. Joel Poremba uncovered the courageous soul of his father's heroic survival. What makes this harrowing, unimaginable book so powerful is that this survival story is told through the respectful lens of a loving son who helped his father share for us the era of anti-semitism and genocide Nathan Poremba lived through; antisemitism and genocide many today deny took place in Poland. The memoir of Nathan Poremba peers into the mindset of a Jewish boy who did what he had to do to live while so many around him did not, including his own family. Nathan's ability to carry on while simultaneously enveloped without the promise there would be a tomorrow exponentially increased his hardship and tested his will to live. This book shines the light of the human spirit that illuminated the dark world from which Nathan came.

Learning how a child of nine years miraculously survived on his own in a world full of darkness and death conveys an astonishing account of the resilience of Jewish life. Nathan Poremba's fight for life, being his own and best advocate, his undeterred resistance and spirit, no matter what horrors were thrown at him, serve as a lesson on dealing with adversity relevant in modern times. Nathan maintained his own deeply embed-ded Jewish values and identity throughout his six-year experience during the war despite the evil that surrounded him. His endurance enabled him to transmit these values lovingly to his children and grandchildren eventually.

Nathan Poremba's unbelievable inner strength and singular focus have impacted me greatly. Few of us, if any, can relate to having survived the Holocaust, let alone as a young child. Yet, I am sure that all who immerse themselves into this extraordinary work will not only be forever changed by what is shared in these pages but will begin to understand the importance of exploring one's past, sharing one's history and story, no matter how uncomfortable or painful the memories. I could not help but read this book and wonder why bad things befell innocent children.

> "In some ways, suffering ceases to be suffering when it finds a meaning. If there is meaning in life at all, then there must be meaning in suffering. Life is never made unbearable by circumstances, only by lack of meaning and purpose."
> —RABBI JONATHAN SACKS-Z"L

Each one of us stands on the shoulders of history and must continue to challenge ourselves. This powerful story about the Holocaust solidifies the notion of just that one must turn pain into purpose.

I am honored to not only have been asked to write this Foreword but even more so, I am honored to have played a small role in Joel Poremba's spiritual journey, as we trekked together, not long ago, on a men's week-long adventure of discovery throughout the land of Israel, the ancient homeland of the Jewish people. This trip pushed the author over the finish line to finally face his father and tell his Holocaust story.

As a Hollywood filmmaker and movie buff, a great Saturday night tradition in our home is to watch a family movie snuggled together on our couch: me, my wife, and our four kids. Munching on a bowl of hot buttered popcorn, we generally watch classic films such as *Singing in The Rain, E.T., The Sound of Music*, or *The Empire Strikes Back*. However, now that our oldest children have reached their teen years and *The Diary of Anne Frank* and *Night* have been introduced into their school curricula, we, as parents, have agonized as to the appropriate time to introduce the Holocaust to them through films such as *Schindler's List, The Boy in the Striped Pajamas*, and Holocaust documentaries. Though we understand our responsibility and the importance of transmitting this history and challenges faced by the Jewish people over the centuries, we, like many other parents, have also wanted to protect our children for as long as possible from the pain and awareness that antisemitism is alive and well in the 21st century. But with the Nazi Holocaust, those who lived to tell have a duty to share what happened, explain as best they can why it happened so that future generations can guard against its re-occurrence.

Rabbi Noah Weinberg - z"l, founder and visionary of Aish HaTorah, once said, "If you don't know what you are willing to DIE for, then you are not LIVING for anything! So, find what you ARE willing to die for, and now LIVE for it!"

The goal of life cannot merely be cuddling on a couch under a safe, warm blanket watching classic musicals. We must all explore opportunities that help us look beyond our comfort zones, however difficult, all to delve deeper into understanding the historical challenges of a people and try and make those experiences part of who we are. Only then can we grow, and by taking responsibility, ensure a better, safer tomorrow for future generations. The Holocaust story of Nathan Poremba serves as a testament to a fight for life when life seemed to abandon him. It stands as testimony in the reach for the light.

SAUL BLINKOFF
Hollywood producer (former Disney animator/director, producer at DreamWorks Animation and at Netflix); motivational speaker; podcast host of "Life of AWESOME!" http://www.saulblinkoff.com/

PROLOGUE

> "For the survivor who chooses to testify, it is clear:
> his duty is to bear witness for the dead and for the living.
> He has no right to deprive future generations of a past
> that belongs to our collective memory. To forget would be
> not only dangerous but offensive; to forget the dead
> would be akin to killing them a second time."
> —ELIE WIESEL, *NIGHT*

The common definition of "duty" is a moral or legal obligation, or responsibility, to undertake action to realize an established circumstance or goal. Elie Wiesel said it best in describing the duty a Holocaust survivor has. In Wiesel's words, the survivor who decides to come forward and share his/her story takes on a duty. To have weathered the Nazi storm, its genocidal machinations to end European Jewry is but a start. The survivor that chooses to testify must do more than just live. The survivor's job is not complete by merely dusting himself or herself off and thriving in life after the Holocaust. According to Wiesel, to forget what transpired is like killing the dead again.

The Holocaust survivor must bear witness for the dead and the living, for Jew and non-Jew alike. A lesson must be learned lest the crime is committed repeatedly. Without bearing witness and sharing the testimony of what he saw, heard, and felt, it is almost as if none of it happened because not far off, there will be those who deny any of it ever occurred.

The stories of survival against all odds often consist of a winding, long and unpredictable road set against unforeseen obstacles. For Nathan Poremba, one of the challenges was being only nine years old at the outset of the Nazi Holocaust when his father was murdered just twelve days into World War II. The other horrific test he faced was being only eleven years old when his mother was murdered. This death left him all alone and on the run for the next nearly three years.

Nathan Poremba's Shoah story (phonetic, "sho-ah," the Hebrew word for the Holocaust) is as much about survival as it is reliance. It is a story of resistance, persistence, and the undying thirst to live. He was a Holocaust survivor, but he was so much more. He was brave, courageous. By 1942 at age twelve, he had lost his parents and sisters, and by 1945 more than two hundred of an extended family were dead, but he resiliently continued to fight for his life. He did what was required to live: he refused to wear the Star of David armband mandated by law; he snuck in and out of three ghettos and walked in and out of the Krakow Ghetto, mixing in among the Schindler Jews. He obtained false papers, worked on a farm next to a German fortress in Bibice, Poland, and delivered German soldiers dairy products. He was then sent to Bergen-Belsen, and Płaszów concentration camps yet lived to knock on the door of his family home in 1945 when the war was over. Even after the horrors of the Holocaust, he married and had two children of his own. He is ninety-one years old and never once complained. He is a fighter, a hero, and the strongest person you might ever meet and would likely never know he survived the Holocaust.

Nathan witnessed Nazi brutality and genocide along with Polish antisemitism carried out before, during, and after the Holocaust. He also observed and experienced Polish complicity alongside the Nazis. Working in conjunction with each other by design or happenstance, these two forces heaped intolerable cruelty, torture, and hopelessness on Nathan. Despite these evils, Nathan's determination, and opposition to both the Nazi war machine and Polish complicity were buttressed by his parents' modeling before and during the Holocaust. His parents were the bookends to this six-year story that provided the map for how and why he survived the Holocaust.

My Name is Staszek Surdel (phonetic, "Sta-shek Sur-dell") is the story of a small Polish Jewish boy brutally uprooted from his home, terrorized, and torn away from his family, Jewish life, and Jewish identity. His was an experience marked by the cold-blooded murder of his father and painful separation from his mother, who permitted him to run so that it might save him despite her difficult decision to acquiesce to her son's bold request.

This is a story of Jewish endurance against two seemingly immovable forces of evil: one exported from Nazi Germany into Poland and the other sewn into Poland's national psyche long before the war. Together with an enduring spirit to live, Nathan's defiance comprises the blueprint for his survival through the darkest period world Jewry has ever seen. They also set the stage for how he subsequently thrived as a Jew in the United States.

This story traces the Holocaust through the eyes of a nine-year-old who exhibited untold bravery and the ability to adapt. It examines the psychologies a young boy employed and the difficult emotional and physical choices he was compelled to make and often revise on a moment's notice. Alone and without help for most of the Holocaust, Nathan Poremba's six-year survival necessitated avoiding detection while maintaining an unflinching will to live despite the threats that enveloped his every move.

How a Jewish child survived while trapped in Poland, cut-off from his relatives, is detailed against his narrow escapes from genocide. Living next to and on top of a Nazi outpost for a significant period and living to tell about it, his story fulfills the duty imposed by not just Wiesel but all humankind. He is the voice of someone who saw, heard, and stood up to antisemitism and evaded genocide. He lived to tell about it by turning his pain and guilt into purpose. *This is a hero's story.*

INTRODUCTION

"In the last analysis, antisemitism is a religious problem."
—JACQUES MAUDAULE

In the fall of 1997, Pope John Paul II stated, ". . . erroneous and unjust interpretations of the New Testament regarding the Jewish people and their alleged culpability [in the Crucifixion] have circulated for too long . . ." Moreover, those interpretations "contributed to a lulling of many consciences" during World War II such that while there were some "Christians who did everything to save those who were persecuted, even to the point of risking their own lives, [but that] the spiritual resistance of many [other Christians] was not what humanity expected of Christ's disciples."

The Pope's speech was delivered to a Vatican seminar covering anti-Jewish currents in Christian theology. Unfortunately, the Pope's comments stopped well short of confronting the Church's complicity of silence and inaction during the Holocaust. But it did, in small measure, address the basic failings in Christianity's teachings as it concerns world Jewry.

Karol Józef Wojtyła was born in 1920 in Wadowice, Poland. He later became known as Pope John Paul II. He was ten years older than Nathan Poremba when the Holocaust began in 1939. Growing up just thirty-two miles southeast of Kraków, young Karol was likely aware the great city of Kraków was the de facto Jewish capital of the world at that time.

What is less likely is that by 1945 Karol ever knew he would one day become the pope. Or that one day he would offer an apology to world Jewry on behalf of all Christianity. His address was an acknowledgment no pope before him had likely ever contemplated.

What occurred between the dawn of time and 1945 as it concerns the Church's role in anti-Judaism? What transpired between 1945 and 1997 to prompt Pope John Paul II to recognize Christianity's role in global anti-Judaism, especially anti-Judaism historically practiced in his Polish homeland? These topics require separate discussion. The Jewish resistance survival story of Nathan Poremba covers the narrow period of 1930 to 1945.

In some small measure, perhaps, this story explains why the Pope offered his 1997 apology. Without question, Christian behavior, both German and Polish, before, during, and after the Holocaust, justified the basis for an apology.

Nathan Poremba's experiences as the last Jew of Wieliczka very directly offers an idea why the Pope offered his apology.

CHAPTER ONE

A JEWISH CITY IN THE SHADOW
OF KRAKÓW

Wieliczka (phonetic, "Ve-leech-ka") is a small Polish city located approximately eight miles southeast of Kraków. It is approximately five square miles in size. In 1939, and for centuries before, Wieliczka was known for its world-famous salt mine. It was and still is one of the world's oldest operating salt mines, a site of world cultural significance due to its geological uniqueness. Southern Poland was known for its rich potassium and salt deposits, and Wieliczka became the region's salt extraction capital. The first mention of underground salt in Wieliczka is found in writings of 1124, but its industrial utilization began in the 8th decade of the 13th century.[1]

Between the 1920s and 1939, Wieliczka Jews owned most taverns and inns in the city. The same was true of the local timber and grain warehouses. Jews also owned and operated the city's only paper factory. Before World War II, Wieliczka Jews also owners of the local furniture, paint, and textile stores.[2]

Irony often paints a curious landscape. Deep inside the Wieliczka salt mine, the Hebrew phrase for welcome, "Baruch Haba!" had been carved into one wall well before the Holocaust.[3] Today the Wieliczka salt mine includes a health resort underground where patrons spend a night or two

---

1. Shmuel Meiri (ed.), *The Jewish Community of Wieliczka; A Memorial Book*, (Kehilat Wieliczka; Sefer Zikaron), (The Wieliczka Assoc. in Israel, M. Stern Press, 1980), [English version], 7.
2. Ibid., 20.
3. Ibid., 36.

Wieliczka, Poland, Nathan Poremba's home town: just eight miles southeast of Krakow; 181 miles southwest of Warsaw.

The world-famous Wieliczka Salt Mine, approximately 1930. (Polish National Digital Archive, courtesy Narodowe Archiwum Cyfrowe.)

healing various ailments. The healing properties of the salt mine are said to provide a soothing effect on inflammation, namely, aching joints, as they are also said to be effective for respiratory diseases and allergies. A city that presently offers a "healing experience" that had a "welcome!" sign written in Hebrew was once a city of anti-Judaism and intense antisemitism, a city whose citizens proudly participated in round-ups, liquidation, and the mass genocide of its Jews.

Jewish settlement in Wieliczka was not permitted until about 1870.[4] In 1900, the Jewish population of Wieliczka numbered just 981 and comprised about 15% of the population.[5] By 1939, Wieliczka's Jews totaled almost 1,500, nearly all of whom lived in the city.[6] However, the Jewish population in the area was larger. A small town adjacent to Wieliczka and a bit to the southeast named, Klasno, contained an official

4. Shmuel Spector, Geoffrey. Wigoder (eds.), *The Encyclopedia of Jewish Life Before and During the Holocaust* (NYU Press, 2001), 1442; Michael Berenbaum, Fred Skolnik (eds.), *Encyclopedia Judaica* (Macmillan Reference USA in association with the Keter Pub. House, 2007), vol. 16, 242, 496.

5. ChaeRan Freez, Paula E. Hyman, Antony Polonsky (eds.), *Polin: Studies in Polish Jewry* (Liverpool University Press., Littman Library of Jewish Civilization, 2007), vol. 18, 193, fn 15.

6. Geoffrey Megargee, *The United States Holocaust Memorial Museum Encyclopedia of Camps and Ghettos* (Bloomington, Indiana: University of Indiana Press, 2012), vol. 2, 591.

Wieliczka, approximately 1920. (Courtesy of Virtual Shtetl - https://sztetl.org.pl/en/
file/61082?ref=city&nid=322 / POLIN Museum of the History of Polish Jews.)

Jewish living quarter which was associated with, and often included, in
the City of Wieliczka's municipal functions. Most of the Jews living in
and between the Wieliczka / Klasno area actually lived in the Klasno.
Taken together, the total Jewish population of these two sister-towns was
more than 4,000 just before the outbreak of war in 1939. Therefore, the
Jewish community in this area comprised nearly half of the local area's
population.[7] Many small villages and farms surrounded the city where
most Christian Poles lived and worked.

The closest major city to Wieliczka is to the north. In 1939, Kraków
was a city of 250,000 people and was known as the center of Polish
Jewry. Before the war, some 56,000 Jews lived there. Kraków was an
influential center of Jewish spiritual life before the outbreak of the war
with multiple forms of Jewish observance from Orthodox to Hasidic to
Conservative to Reform movements. While there were at least 90 shuls
(synagogues) in Kraków before the German invasion of Poland in 1939,
Wieliczka had a much smaller Jewish population but remained a viable
Jewish community. Thus, even though Wieliczka was a relatively new

7. https://www.belzec.eu/en/page/deportations/238;
https://sztetl.org.pl/en/towns/w/322-wieliczka/99-history/138230-history-of-community.

Jewish settlement, its infrastructure supporting Jewish life had come a long way in a noticeably short period.

Wieliczka Jews enjoyed living outside the hustle and bustle of Kraków but were still close enough to feel connected to the larger Jewish community. Larger shuls, markets, and yeshivot (education institutions focused on studying religious texts, primarily Talmud and Torah) dotted the landscape in Kraków. Wieliczka was parceled into the District of Kraków.

Before the war, Nathan's father, Joseph Poremba, drove a bus between Wieliczka and Katowice. Katowice is a small Polish town about an hour northwest of Wieliczka and passed Kraków. The bus Joseph drove held twenty-four seats. To get around Wieliczka in the 1930s, Poles either walked, traveled by horse-and-buggy, or, on one of a dozen or so city buses. Only one privately-owned car was known to exist in Wieliczka before the war. As a result, the people of Wieliczka relied heavily on city buses to get to the train station in Wieliczka, from where most people traveled to other parts of Poland. From there most traveled to and from Warsaw and Kraków.

Nathan's mother, Gustava Poremba, owned and worked in her tavern, or *shenk*, in Wieliczka. The *shenk* sold sandwiches, Polska kielbasa, beer, and vodka. The local salt miners and farmers from just outside of the city were the tavern's most frequent and loyal customers. Before the war, the store was always busy, serving Jews and non-Jews alike without incident. The floor was comprised of creaky wooden planks, many of them uneven but covered with a thick coating of sawdust. Wooden beams ran from the floor to the roof and across the inside ceiling to form a lattice design. There were two stoves in the center of the floor which provided the only heat for the tavern.

The tavern attracted more textile workers, salt miners, and farmers outside the city than doctors, lawyers, and academics. The patrons were mostly civil to each other and Gustava. Shift workers physically tired from their work wanted only to enjoy food, drink, and each other's company.

Despite the peace provided in Gustava's *shenk*, Wieliczka experienced its share of anti-Jewish riots. By the end of the 19th century, the conflicts between Wieliczka's Jews and its non-Jewish residents increased. Violent

Outdoor town market in Wieliczka, approximately 1930. (Polish National Digital Archive, courtesy Narodowe Archiwum Cyfrowe.)

riots against the city's Jews took place in 1889 and 1906.[8] Even more took place between 1914 and 1920.[9] As antisemitism became more prevalent in Poland in the 1920s and 1930s, such incidents also increased in Wieliczka. Polish antisemitism saw a huge spike in incidents after World War I.

After World War I, Poland became a democratic, independent state. Various minorities chose to emigrate to Poland, including Ukrainians, Belorussians, Lithuanians, and ethnic Germans. Jews from these areas also migrated to Poland. They sought the promises of economic freedom in Poland and the prospects of making a home that was free from the political entanglements the prior war attracted in their former homelands. However, increasing Polish nationalism and resulting hostility towards newcomers made the country an extremely dangerous place for Jewish immigrants. There were both pogroms and discriminatory laws

8. Spector, *The Encyclopedia of Jewish Life Before and During the Holocaust*, 1442.
9. William W. Hagen, *Anti-Jewish Violence in Poland, 1914–1920* (Cambridge University Press, 2018), 102–108.

against Jews, which provided signs of a growing wave of antisemitism in Poland after World War I.[10]

But the calm that once existed in Wieliczka slowly gave way.

Nathan was nine years old when World War II began. In the nine years leading up to the war, Wieliczka became a city where it was *always* "open season" on Jews. It was commonplace for Poles to chase Jews home from work and school. Nathan witnessed this near daily. He saw Christian Poles throw rocks at Jews and beat them in the city streets almost every day. Most often, onlookers stood, cheered, and did nothing to intervene. At least once a week in public, Nathan heard anti-Jewish slurs from Poles when they spoke about their Jewish co-workers, schoolmates, or neighbors. He regularly saw anti-Jewish graffiti and banners around town, which was often sanctioned and permitted by local city officials. This was the Wieliczka that Nathan grew up in. While his first nine years of life saw no war, it was certainly marked by many anti-Jewish incidents.

Anti-Jewish bias was no stranger to the court system either. The city's Jews lost most business disputes with Wieliczka Poles in court. When civil cases went to court, and a Jew was a party litigant to a civil action, he or she often faced anti-Jewish judges. Most often, Jewish litigants lost in front of a jury comprised mostly of Christian Poles. In court, if a Jew was a party, his or her religion was repeated by the opposing attorneys or the judge. This way, the jury was constantly reminded a Jew was before it. Where a legal matter was criminal, the accused Jewish defendant was nearly always found guilty. The jury or judge often disregarded exculpating evidence. Well before the war, the theme in Wieliczka was to "get the Jew," which occurred both in and out of a court of law.

Nathan could not remember a time growing up in Wieliczka when antisemitism and anti-Jewish sentiment were not rampant. Officials did nothing to discourage it. In fact, they encouraged it. Most priests in Wieliczka were openly anti-Jewish as well.

But, like nearly all Polish Jews, Nathan had little idea that in a few years, anti-Judaism would develop into mass genocide. Few Polish Jews foresaw life being worse than what they had tolerated for so long.

---

10. Richard J. Evans, *The Third Reich at War* (Penguin Press, 2010), 49.

A KOSHER HOME

Joseph Poremba ("Yosef" or "Josef") was born in 1896 in Miechów, Poland, twenty-four miles northeast of Kraków. Gustawa Poremba, ("Gustava" or "Gustav"), (nee Lewkowicz; phonetic, "Lefkovitz"), was born in 1899 in Wieliczka, Poland. The two married in approximately 1918 and rented a small home. They had five children: Tala ("Natalia" or "Talia"); Esta ("Esther"); Sala; Fela ("Felicia"); and Natan ("Natak" or "Nathan"), the lone boy.

Nathan was born January 25, 1930, and named *Natan ben Yosef* ("Nathan, son of Yosef").

With two steady incomes, Nathan's family were middle to upper-middle-class by Wieliczka standards. The family of five lived comfortably relative to other Poles.

In 1936 or 1937, Nathan's parents bought a new brick home located at Reymonta #8. It had two finished bedrooms, a kitchen, two basements, and a large attic that could be made into one or two extra rooms. In addition, Nathan's childhood home had running water, a toilet located inside the home, and electricity, all luxuries at that time. Such amenities were rare for many Polish homes in the 1930s located outside a major Polish city.

The Porembas were conservative/orthodox Jews. In today's vernacular, they could best be described as "conservadox" given their custom, practice, and level of religious observance. Gustava kept a kosher home and prepared the Shabbos meal every Friday night. She always lit Shabbos candles with her daughters. In addition, she cooked Shabbos fish, chicken, and soup every Friday night. The family kept the Sabbath and went to shul every Friday night and Saturday morning. In the living room, Joseph maintained a small hutch with several shelves of books. Several tractates, or portions, of the Talmud, lined half a shelf, the Five Books of Moses, or Torah, the rest of the same shelf. Below that shelf sat Shabbat candles, a menorah, and a Chanukiah. Next to the bookcase were two chairs where Gustava and Joseph typically sat on either end of a small table and lamp. A small sofa sat across from the table is where one or more of the children would sit and chat with their parents.

Nathan had one toy growing up. It was a four-foot-long miniature car with a seat for two, a set of foot pedals, and a steering wheel. Joseph bought the toy car when Nathan was about seven years old. Most children in 1930s Wieliczka did not have toys, nor did most kids in pre-war Poland. Before the war, Nathan spent more time outside playing with friends than he did inside the house. Almost all his friends were Jewish and lived within a few blocks of his home. All the families knew one another and attended the same shul.

By the late 1920s, Wieliczka Jews tended not to depend on their non-Jewish neighbors in the way neighbors typically do. Slowly disappearing were the old neighborly attitudes: borrowing flour or sugar, sharing stories outside, or chasing down a loose ball belonging to a next-door neighbor. Front doors were all too often slammed in the face of a Jewish neighbor seeking a spare hammer or nails to borrow. By the early 1930s, the Jews of Wieliczka tended to stay mostly among their own.

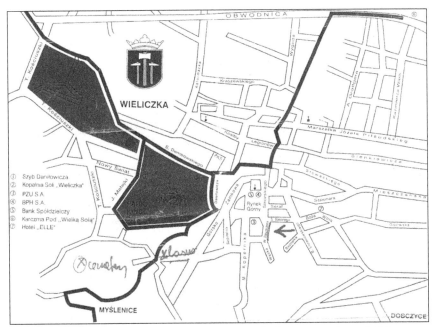

Reymonta Street (dark arrow), where the Poremba's Wieliczka home was located. (Map acquired by Nathan Poremba in the 1980s showing where the nearby Klasno Jewish cemetery was in relation to his home; handwriting is his own.)

It did not take long before Wieliczka Jews were forced to limit even more of their interactions with Christian Poles. As Nazi xenophobia and (racial) antisemitism increased, it began to spill into Poland and eventually to Wieliczka. By the mid-1930s, Wieliczka's Jewish community was experiencing heightened antisemitism, as were Jews throughout Poland. Where once Wieliczka Jews frequented open markets and publicly interacted with their Christian neighbors, this came to a standstill by the mid-1930s. Joseph, ever cognizant of this, often discussed Wieliczka's mounting animosity with his family.

Joseph came from a large family in Miechów and was one of ten siblings. More than two hundred family members went by "Poremba" on Joseph's side of the family. He often took Nathan along to visit his large family in Miechów, the two of them alone. As Joseph's only son, whenever Nathan arrived, he was routinely fussed over and showered with attention. Visiting with his dozens of aunts and uncles and playing with his first cousins in Miechów was a welcome treat for Nathan. Without any brothers of his own, these visits provided Nathan with camaraderie and demonstrated to him he came from a large, proud Jewish family. Nathan was closest to his maternal grandmother, Helen Channah Lewkowicz (also known as "Mary L. Ringer"), who lived with Nathan's family in Wieliczka. Because

Gustava; Sala; Nathan; Fela; Esta; Tala; and Joseph Poremba, circa 1931, (left to right), one of two pre-war family photographs discovered after the Holocaust.

no other Porembas lived in Wieliczka, whenever Nathan was in Miechów, he felt safer there because so many family members surrounded him. As anti-Judaism morphed into antisemitism in Wieliczka, the absence of family members increased concern about his family's safety.

The shul to which Nathan and his family belonged did not have electricity and instead relied on candles for its light. The synagogue members supplied their own candles and would kindle them outside of the shul before going in. There were stands attached to the backside of the pews where the lit candles rested. This was the only way the light was provided in the synagogue. The women sat upstairs, separated from the men down below. Most of their Christian neighbors treated the shul with respect, and so the shul was a safe, warm, and welcoming spiritual home for the Porembas. The three shuls in Wieliczka were relatively free of anti-Semitic incidents, the few places in town that did not see many open hostilities from local Poles before the war.

The face of the city changed in observance of holy days. All work for Jews came to a halt. Jewish shops closed early; business transactions

Post-war photo of the conservative shul the Porembas attended in Klasno, southwest of Wieliczka, located on Wiejska Street 11 (formerly Berka Joselewicza Street). (Courtesy Daniel Zawadzki via Virtual Shtetl - www.sztetl.org.pl.)

stopped by sundown and remained closed until the Shabbos or the holiday ended. Nobody desecrated the Shabbos as nearly every Jew in Wieliczka was observant. Nathan and his father did not go to shul every day during the week, but when Shabbat or any Jewish holiday arrived, Joseph took Nathan to shul. The two customarily held hands walking to their shul in Klasno, a nearby town just south of Wieliczka, the ultra-conservative synagogue which the family belonged to. The synagogue was built in the mid-18th Century in Klasno within the historical borders of Siercza. It was a weekly tradition that they both looked forward to as they would always walk to shul ahead of the four women in the family. For Wieliczka Jews, Klasno was its proud sister city to the southwest.

In 1938, the rabbi of the Klasno synagogue began openly discussing the growing menace to the west, Nazi Germany, and the increasing antisemitism in Poland. Even though he was only eight years old, Nathan was aware of the increasing tension and wary among the adults even though he did not know exactly what it meant.

There were several kosher markets and eateries in Wieliczka for the Jewish community. Most of the kosher goods were shipped in daily from Kraków. But a *mikveh*, (a ritual bathhouse to achieve purity), was located in Klasno. As a "townlet," Klasno had been previously incorporated into Wieliczka in 1924. This was where the Jewish cemetery and *mikveh* were located, also within walking distance to Wieliczka.

Before the war, Nathan attended school at the local *cheder* (phonetic, "ch-Hay-der" or Jewish school where the basics of Judaism and Hebrew were taught) from age three to five. There he learned the *alef beis* (the Hebrew alphabet, or "A-B-Cs"), studied the Jewish holidays, and was taught Hebrew songs. Hebrew and Yiddish were spoken at the *cheder* along with Polish.

While Polish Jews played a dominant role in the developing economy of Poland, particularly in the development of commerce and higher education, many Christians in Wieliczka resented the Jews and their role in the town's economy. In particular, the contributions of Wieliczka Jews did not sit well with the local clergy, who stoked hate between the local Christians and Jews. It was always beginning with traditional enmity as the crucifiers of their messiah. Both the upper, middle, and lower classes of Polish society looked to stifle Jews through pogroms, boycotts, harsh edicts, restrictions on where Jews could live, and libel.[11] As a result, the Jews of Wieliczka lived under the threat of boycotts, higher taxes and fees, and other restrictions.

Roman Dmowski was a Polish statesman and a prominent leader of Poland's struggle for national liberation. In 1893, he founded Liga Narodowa (the National League), a subversive organization of Polish nationalists. Dmowski's writings often promoted the belief of an "international Jewish conspiracy" aimed against Poland.[12] Polish anti-Judaism certainly predated Dmowski, but he took it to another level in the 19th century and paved the way for Polish antisemitism. For example, in his essay about World War I, "Żydzi wobec wojny" ("Jews on the War"), Dmowski claimed that Zionism was only a cloak to disguise the Jewish ambition to rule the world.[13] Well before the Holocaust, Dmowski sought a Jew-free Poland, a position he held for all 3,000,000 Jewish Poles.[14] He was also a fervent advocate of boycotts of Jewish business.[15]

While not in the majority political party, Dmowski's ideology ran deep in Poland. To illustrate the effect Dmowski's writings had before the war, even post-war Poland saw fit to honor him. In 2007 the county erected a sixteen-foot bronze statue of Dmowski in Warsaw, where it still stands today. Moreover, Dmowski's influence is so deeply rooted in Poland's psyche that in 2018 the Polish government issued a new passport design that featured Dmowski's image.

Such was life in Wieliczka before the war. Dmowski's voice and antisemitic positions became the dominant ideology in Wieliczka: boycotts of Jewish businesses and defamatory rhetoric about Jews "ruling the world." Before the Nazis ever arrived, the groundwork had been laid that made for an effortless policy transition from an anti-Jewish Wieliczka to much more of an antisemitic city. Contrary to Dmowski's erroneous notions that Zionism was solely about Jewish ambition for a take-over

11. Meiri, *The Jewish Community of Wieliczka*, 9–10.

12. Rafal Pankowski, *The Populist Radical Right in Poland: The Patriots* (Routledge, 2010), 26.

13. Roman Dmowski, *Polityka Polska i odbudowanie państwa* ("Polish Politics and the Rebuilding of the State"), (1925), 301–308.

14. Gunnar Paulsson, *Secret City: The Hidden Jews of Warsaw*, 1940–1945 (Yale University Press, 2002), 38.

15. Andrzej Walicki, "The Troubling Legacy of Roman Dmowski," *East European Politics & Societies* (December 1999, vol. 14), 28–29.

of the world, Wieliczka's thriving Zionist movement was committed to a singular purpose: the re-establishment of the Land of Israel. Wieliczka's own Zionist movement saw tremendous participation between the two World Wars as youth movements were organized, wide-ranging cultural programs offered and participation therein expanded.[16]

A gathering of members of the Hashomer Ha'Tzair movement in Wieliczka, Poland, May 18, 1939 (Courtesy Yad Vashem Photo Archives No. 4197/1 https://www.yadvashem.org/holocaust/this-month/may/1939-2.html).

---

16. Meiri, *The Jewish Community of Wieliczka*, 29–32.

CHAPTER TWO

ANTISEMITISM IN WIELICZKA, 1935–1939

ALTERCATION WITH A CHAMPION POLISH WRESTLER

One day in 1935, Joseph fired up his bus and began his usual daily route. Up to this point, he had never once experienced an anti-Jewish or anti-semitic incident while driving his bus. He had witnessed plenty of such incidents in Wieliczka, but while in his uniform, behind the wheel, he had been treated with respect.

But on this day, a well-known Polish wrestler boarded Joseph's bus. The wrestler was famous in Wieliczka as a past national champion and was well known for his antisemitism. The brute entered the bus without paying the fare. The wrestler could certainly afford the bus fare, but he intended to pick a fight with a bus driver whom he knew to be Jewish. In pre-war Wieliczka, a small city, Christian Poles knew who their Jewish neighbors were.

The champion wrestler's antisemitism had been well-covered in Polish newspapers while he was active on the wrestling circuit. Even though he was retired, Joseph knew exactly who the wrestler was when he boarded. From his body language, Joseph knew precisely why the man chose not to pay his fare. He was fixing for a confrontation with Joseph.

Joseph was not going to let a man who could afford to pay simply ride for free. So, Joseph put the bus in park, motor idling. He stood up from his seat, turned around, and took a few steps down the aisle towards the wrestler. He calmly requested the fare from the wrestler several times, but the man refused, took his seat, and only glared back. After a few uncomfortable seconds, the wrestler yelled, "*Zhyd! Zhyd!*" ("Jew-boy! Jew-boy!"), daring Joseph to do something.

Joseph sat back down and turned off the bus's engine. He stood up, informed his passengers the bus was not moving until the wrestler paid or exited the bus. Nothing changed. No one budged. A few more seconds of awkward silence went by, only to be broken as the wrestler continued with another round of anti-Semitic slurs.

Joseph then walked off the bus, motioned to the wrestler that he should follow him outside. The wrestler was all too happy to oblige. He must have counted on having an easy physical brawl with Joseph. The wrestler walked back up the bus aisle and gloated to the other passengers that he would kill Joseph. As the aggressor stepped off the bus, Joseph asked him once more for the fare. The wrestler shook his head "no." Joseph then lunged at the large man, wrapping his hands around the back of his neck, and threw him to the ground. The two engaged in a violent fight that left the wrestler savagely beaten and unconscious. Joseph was also terribly injured, but the fight ended with him still standing, and the wrestler knocked flat on his back. Joseph managed to get back on his bus and finish his shift before returning home to nurse his injuries.

Once word of the incident spread, officials from the city decided to pull Joseph's license and work permit. City authorities ruled the license and permit would never be reinstated. It ruled there would be no hearing or investigation into the incident. They made this ruling without hearing a word from Joseph or any witnesses on the bus. The wrestler went to the local newspaper to report the fight to buttress his well-established anti-semitic reputation and created a story about saving patrons from having to listen to a Jewish driver. Of course, the newspaper article made Joseph out to be the aggressor and instigated the fight. The wrestler also told the paper he paid his bus fare and stated that Joseph fought him because he did not like Christians. He also concealed that he had called Joseph "Jew boy!" but without interviewing any bus witnesses, there was no one to set the account straight. Public opinion was rarely, if ever, going to take the side of a Polish Jew in 1935, let alone in Wieliczka.

To cement its anti-Jewish reputation, the city backed the wrestler's story because he was a national icon, and on the other side of the equation sat a Jew. It also burnished city officials' reputation as it was beneficial to the city government to support a famous anti-Jewish man while adversely impacting a Jew's livelihood. It made them look decisive as having taken "action" against a Jew. The city authorities blacklisted Joseph and prohibited him from ever working for the city in any capacity.

With his city job eliminated, the two-income family was suddenly reduced to one. After a long recovery, Joseph went to work with Gustava in her tavern.

ASSAULTS IN PUBLIC SCHOOL

Nathan had experienced some anti-Judaism during his first six years of life, but nothing was directed at him personally. But his father's earlier bold courage in confronting the wrestler acted to shape Nathan's character.

How Nathan dealt with antisemitism at a young age foreshadowed how he would come to confront it during the Holocaust. It was inexplicable a six-year-old would be charged with fully comprehending anti-Jewish attitudes and incidents of antisemitism. But Nathan's early experiences with both in Wieliczka taught him how to cope and work around it. His early brushes with antisemitism in Wieliczka taught him not to succumb, not to cower, but rather to react to it with self-preservation in mind. The ability to confront it foretold instincts that were traceable to his father.

When he was six years old, Nathan was refused continued enrollment at the *cheder*. The headmaster informed Gustava that Nathan should sit out a year and come back for first grade when he was physically bigger. Nathan was short for a six-year-old and had a small frame. The headmaster simply would not enroll him until he had grown more. By not acquiescing to hold her son out of school for a year, Gustava decided to look at secular schooling. Unbeknown to her, this decision would ultimately aid Nathan in developing survival skills no one conceived he might ever need.

Gustava did not see any value in Nathan staying at home for a year and missing out on school. She told the headmaster she would not keep him at home, merely hoping he would grow taller by the next year. This was wasted time to his mother. So Gustava decided Nathan would be better off in a public school for a year. After that, he could return to the *cheder* for a second showing after meeting the headmaster's bizarre height requirement.

Gustava soon discovered that Nathan would be the only Jewish student in the entire public school. In a small town where everyone knew everybody, Christian Polish school children knew who was Jewish. Thus, by the end of his first day of first grade, the news had spread that a new student was amongst them and that he was Jewish. Beginning with his second day, the teachers ordered Nathan to sit in the back of the class simply because he was Jewish. They told him a Jew sits in the back of the class.

By the third day, and every day after that, Nathan was slapped, punched, and elbowed to the back of his head as his Christian classmates took their seats. As they passed his seat, his classmates called Nathan "*żydowski szczur*" ("Jewish rat"), and they harassed him on the playground during lunch. Nathan complained to his teachers and the school principal, but they did not act to curb the attacks. Resigned to help himself, Nathan took to solving the problem. He decided it would only make matters worse if he had told his parents about the abuse. He instead chose to devise his own solution.

The plan went like this: every day, Gustava gave Nathan a few pennies to buy ice cream or a candy bar for the walk home from school. Instead of spending the money on snacks, Nathan decided to forego the sweets and offer the money to the classmate who hit him the hardest. This bully also seemed to dislike Nathan the most for being Jewish. By the end of the second week of school, Nathan approached the boy and asked if he would protect him. The boy laughed at him, but when Nathan offered his few pennies, to be paid every day, the boy enthusiastically agreed and took the job.

For the rest of the year, the boy told his fellow students to leave Nathan alone. However, he protected Nathan when others still dared to attack him.

This arrangement lasted the entire first grade. Nathan's quick-thinking solution made the school year bearable, even if it was not at the *cheder*.

ANTISEMITIC BANNERS AND PLACARDS

Over his first nine years, Nathan had seen antisemitic banners and graffiti routinely all around Wieliczka. Once every twelve to eighteen months, Christian Poles obtained permission to stoke anti-Jewish stereotypes and propagate antisemitism. In the 1930s, this was ritual for the Jews of Wieliczka. The Wieliczka police always protected these hateful expressions, most often sanctioned by the city officials. Notably, during this time, national boycotts and confiscation of Jewish businesses became increasingly more commonplace. The Polish government openly shared its position that its Jewish minority hindered Poland's economic and cultural development, despite all evidence to the contrary. The pre-war Polish government, local and national, rarely, if ever, took responsibility

Joseph and Gustava Poremba (front row arrows, left to right) and, Tala and Esta Poremba (middle row arrows, left to right), in 1937 or 1938, at a Jewish family wedding in Wieliczka, Poland.

for its own failed policies choosing instead to blame Polish Jews. In early 1937 Poland's foreign minister, Józef Beck, declared that Poland could only stand to keep 500,000 Jews and that over the next thirty years, 80,000-100,000 Jews every year would be made to leave Poland.[1] It became national policy to think about shrinking the number of Jews in Poland in the late 1930s.

In May 1939, the City of Wieliczka once again began to harass its Jewish population. The city authorities permitted Christian Poles to put up antisemitic banners on Jewish-owned businesses and government buildings between roadways. The banners draped across the city's thoroughfares contained stereotypical libel messages such as "Jews: Christ-killers" and "Jews Eat Christian Children." In addition, placards placed on Jewish shop windows read "Jews are not Poles," "Jews are Cancer," and "Jews Leave Poland Now!" Nathan saw city employees erected many of the banners with the local policemen in May 1939.

One day in mid-May, Joseph had simply had enough. After the banners and signs had been left up for a few days, Joseph told Nathan to walk with him and watch. "Where are you going?" Nathan asked. "Come with me and see," Joseph said. Joseph decided he would tear down as many banners and placards as he could while people were busy at Sunday mass.

Joseph and a Jewish friend with a ladder went store-by-store, building-by-building, and removed many of the signs. They even took down the larger signs stretched over city roads, even the one put up on a nearby hill. One policeman who liked Joseph chose not to arrest him as Joseph cut ropes and tore down the antisemitic signs. The policeman followed Joseph around and quietly begged him to stop before a riot broke out, but Joseph refused. The policeman then tried to scare Joseph by saying, "they'll beat you, and I am only one officer and cannot overcome a crowd to protect you." Joseph nevertheless kept moving storefront-to-storefront, tearing signs from the windows of Jewish-owned shops. "Joseph, they'll kill you for doing this," the officer pleaded. "I am not afraid," Joseph

---

1. Norman Goda, *The Holocaust: Europe, the World, and the Jews*, 1918–1945 (Taylor & Francis, 2012), 73–74.

replied. Joseph kept removing banners, unafraid as Nathan followed him around from sign-to-sign, watching his father remove the placards.

When church services ended that Sunday, a crowd gathered near the ladder Joseph was standing on. They watched him remove a banner and said nothing. No murmuring, no chatter, not one word of interference or criticism was hurled at Joseph. The policeman who had followed Joseph told the small group of Christians that Joseph had been removing banners all morning. It was hard to know if the policeman was complimenting Joseph or trying to rile them up. Either way, the small group was stunned and left speechless by what they witnessed. A few neighbors that knew him even applauded Joseph.

This was a rare moment of solidarity between Christians and a courageous Jew. Nathan took it all in, but he was unsure what to make of the crowd's passive compliance and tempered applause. Either way, Nathan saw his father react and publicly take a stand against antisemitism once again.

There was no punishment exacted on Joseph by officials, and there was no riot due to what he did that day. This had a profound effect on Nathan, who witnessed his father confront antisemitism. He attentively understood that there might be times when defying hate exacts a price, like when the wrestler fought, injured his father, and he lost his job. But there may be times that an act of defiance is respected and does not cause an altercation, like when his father removed the anti-Jewish signs put up around the city.

The history of anti-Jewish incidents in Wieliczka in the 1920s and 1930s before the Holocaust was laid a dangerous foundation for Jews. In the years growing up, hostility towards Jews was common. Joseph told Nathan many stories of local attacks on Jews, on secular and observant Jews alike. They had stones thrown at them; they were kicked and spat upon. In not one instance did Nathan recall a story from his father where a Wieliczka Jew fought his attacker back. All the stories ended with the Jew running away. But Joseph Poremba was different. So was his son, Nathan.

CHAPTER THREE

A LION OF JUDAH: A FATHER'S FEARLESS LEADERSHIP

During the 1920s and 1930s, Joseph Poremba was among the most respected and well-liked persons in Wieliczka. He was a leader of the Jewish community. Gentiles respected and feared him because he stood up to anti-Semitic incidents and prevented others from escalating. Another way of saying it was that Christian Poles restricted themselves from any anti-Jewish practices in his presence. Few challenged his authoritative and calming presence.

When Joseph walked down a street, Poles could be heard whispering "here he comes" to caution others to cease making antisemitic remarks. Conversely, when Nathan walked down a street alone in Wieliczka or with his Jewish friends, he heard the slurs and curses aimed at him and his friends. But where Joseph Poremba walked around, there would be no such talk.

Part of the reason for this was Joseph having stood up to and confronted the champion wrestler. He was not going to permit public displays of antisemitism where he could prevent it. Some of the respect he received was due to his decision to pull down anti-Jewish and antisemitic banners.

But the main reason Christian Poles stood up straight around Joseph Poremba was that he was a polite, plain-speaking, fair-minded, and physically imposing man. He was much larger than the average Wieliczka Pole. He was stood 6'3" and was 220 pounds, strong as an ox. He had dark hair, an olive complexion, and spoke with a warm, deep voice. He

Lion of Judah, "Aryeh Yehudah," by Israeli scribal artist Kalman Gavriel, "The Jerusalem Scribe," Jerusalem, Israel. (Courtesy Kalman Gavriel.)

led by example and taught Nathan that they would not be made to feel like outsiders by their own neighbors.

He taught Nathan to stand up to antisemitism, never to turn or run from it.

In the 1920s and 1930s, Polish teenagers in Wieliczka often harassed Jewish kids, chasing them and yelling anti-Jewish epithets. When Joseph would come upon such an attack, and it would immediately cease. Sometimes a Polish shopkeeper would claim to have been paid less than the total bill and attempt to create a ruckus in front of a Polish crowd when he had a Jewish customer. If Joseph were near, he would never hesitate to intervene and determine who the offending party really was. Many times, Nathan saw his father intervene and witnessed the shopkeeper yield. Joseph also stepped into fights where Poles outnumbered a Jew. These incidents nearly always broke up upon sight of Nathan's father.

The local police also respected Joseph and were aware of his influence. Wieliczka Jews knew that as long as Joseph was around, trouble could only go so far. Nathan was among those who felt safer when Joseph stepped into the crosshairs of an anti-Semitic incident. With a Lion of Judah in their corner, Jews in Wieliczka felt safer.

Nathan took careful notes of his father's stature and place in the Jewish and Christian communities. He witnessed unruly Poles silence themselves when his father appeared.

Nothing could have prepared Nathan and his family for the coming Nazi storm. Like most of Poland's Jews, and particularly a little boy, Nathan had scant capacity to understand the magnitude of the incoming Nazi terror machine or the genocide it would visit on Poland. Seemingly arriving overnight, the antisemitism of Nazi Germany would dwarf what Jews had been enduring in Poland for many decades.

CHAPTER FOUR

THE SHOAH DESCENDS
UPON WIELICZKA

NEIGHBOR'S RADIO BLASTED HITLER'S
1939 PRE-WAR SPEECHES

The neighbors to the right of Nathan's childhood home were pleasant and friendly people. They were kind in the way good neighbors usually are. The neighbors knew the Porembas were Jewish, but they never showed any sign of antisemitism.

Starting in 1938, Nathan heard the neighbor radio playing loudly through their open windows. For more than a year, Nathan heard their radio tuned to a Polish station that covered Hitler's speeches broadcast into Poland. They were in German with simultaneous Polish translation. To a non-Jew, perhaps the main takeaways from Hitler's prewar speeches might have been the alleged virtues and successes of National Socialism, complaints about the Treaty of Versailles and obsession with defeating Bolshevism. But to a Jew, Hitler's speeches were much more provocative and frightening.

As an eight and nine year old, Nathan did not understand very much German, but he heard Hitler repeatedly scream *"Jude! Jude! Jude!"* in his many speeches, followed by raucous applause and screams for more of such rhetoric. Nathan knew enough to know why the word *"Jude!"* was repeated over and over with unmatched animus. Before and after these speeches, he could hear Polish commentators summarizing the speech's significance to Europe and, particularly, to Poland. During that year, the neighbors never acted any differently to the Porembas despite regularly listening to Hitler's speeches. The neighbors never spoke to the Porembas about Hitler or his ideas. Nor did the Poremba family ever engage their neighbors in a discussion about Hitler's speeches.

Hitler's famous "Reichstag Speech" on January 30, 1939, marked a turning point for Europe and its Jews. It demonstrated the Nazi transition from racial antisemitism toward genocide. It was a speech widely discussed in the Wieliczka Jewish community which received a lot of attention in the Polish press and government. In this speech, Hitler declared that in the event of war in Europe, it would mean the end of European Jewry. While the speech certainly rattled the sword and set out Hitler's justification for a war, one thing was clear: Hitler was fixated on eliminating Europe's Jewish population.

Nathan heard this speech blaring from his neighbor's radio and understood from the Polish commentators what Hitler had said. The speech prophesized, almost thirsted for, the destruction of Europe's Jewish population and worried Polish Jews in and outside of Wieliczka. But to a nine-year-old, Germany was far away, even if it was a country just immediately to the west. Hitler's grandiose speech sounded far-fetched to a little boy incapable of understanding what was going on outside of his small town. He was too young to appreciate the looming threat. It also sounded unreal to most Polish Jews.

In 1938 and early 1939, two significant things began to happen in Poland, particularly in Wieliczka.

First, Polish Jewish newspapers began writing articles about Germany's Nuremberg Laws in increasing frequency. These anti-Semitic laws, codified by the Nazi Reichstag and enacted on September 15, 1935, suddenly felt threatening to them even if they were implemented in Germany. When coupled with increasing Polish radio coverage of Hitler's anti-Semitic speeches in the late 1930s, Nazism's ideological tentacles increasingly spilled over Germany's borders into Poland. Meanwhile, some Polish government officials ratcheted up their own brand of anti-semitism. There was much discussion in Wieliczka about whether Poland might enact their own version of the Nuremberg laws.

Second, German Jews began to emigrate to Poland, with many settling in Wieliczka. They brought with them first-hand stories of Nazi deportations of Jews to German labor camps, midnight Gestapo abductions of Jews, and *Kristallnacht* (the "Night of Broken Glass") on November 9–10, 1938. The new German emigres came with stories of pogroms and the German outlawing of Jewish businesses. The immigrants explained to Polish Jews that Hitler's race laws and resettlement campaign were putting German Jews out of business, banning them from work, and stripping them of their citizenship. All while hundreds of synagogues were destroyed, and Jews were prohibited from attending school.

Polish Jews believed the stories their German kin told. But for many Jewish Poles, the troubles in Nazi Germany seemed more theoretical than real. Only a small minority of Polish Jews saw the coming storm and left Poland for neighboring Eastern European countries. Some left for France and England, but the overwhelming majority remained. Most of Poland's Jews refused to be uprooted by a foreign dictator's evil rhetoric and antisemitism.

During this time, the Porembas had one family discussion about possibly leaving Poland. During the second Passover Seder in April 1939, they discussed recent newspaper articles in the Jewish press and about the alarming events in Nazi Germany. They talked about the Nazi pogroms, roundups, detentions in local jails and German concentration camps. The family was most definitely concerned. But what could they do?

Gustava had a brother in New York City who had relocated there from Poland just before World War I. In late 1938, knowing what was transpiring in Germany, her brother wrote a letter to Gustava imploring the Porembas to come to America. But Gustava's mother was too sick to make such a trek, and Gustava would not leave her behind.

In what would foreshadow Gustava's later actions, she asked her husband, Joseph, to take the five children with him and go to her brother in America. But Joseph would not have it. He refused to split the family up and leave his wife and mother-in-law behind. Besides, he said, he was not going to run from antisemitism in Poland. Little did he know Nazism and genocide were coming with Germany's version of antisemitism and shocking rhetoric of eliminating European Jewry.

SECRET NAZI RECRUITMENT OF A
WIELICZKA MUNICIPAL CLERK

The Nazi invasion of Poland began on September 1, 1939. Within a few days, Wieliczka's Jewish males were ordered to report to clean the city square. In addition, they were ordered to prepare Wieliczka for a "proper greeting" for the Germans. The city order was ironic because Poland was supposed to be repelling the Nazi invasion, but curiously Wieliczka city officials were instead planning to greet their invaders by ordering Jews to clean the city square. The early realization Jews should clean Wieliczka's square for a foreign invader was evidence this was just the beginning of the complicity between Germany and city officials.

On September 7th, the Germans reached Wieliczka. Between September 1st and the 7th, most Jewish men living in and around Wieliczka had already fled. Most Jewish males headed to Kraków, where they felt they could better hide and blend into the population of a much larger city. But Joseph refused to flee. By staying, he demonstrated to his own family he would not abandon them. He reiterated to his family that he was not afraid of the Nazis and that they, too, should remain calm. However, the city order required Jews to collect and remove the horse dung from Nazi horses and put them into their pockets. This order immediately caused most Wieliczka Jews to flee the city.[1] But not Joseph, who complied with the order and did the required work.

The Wehrmacht, the German armed forces, was first into Wieliczka on the 7th. This Wehrmacht unit immediately began a near daily ritual of rounding up Wieliczka's Jewish males in the main marketplace for the purpose of humiliating them in front of their cheering Polish neighbors. The Wehrmacht did this between September 7 and 11, 1939, photographed and documented by their own soldiers. The Germans ordered the Jewish men to sweep the square and to pick up horse dung with their bare hands, putting the dung in buckets and sometimes their pockets.

---

1. Meiri, *The Jewish Community of Wieliczka*, 36.

The Wehrmacht rounded up more than 43 Wieliczka Jewish men in front of Rynek Górny 4, 5 and 6 on a date between September 7-11, 1939. Under the German's orders, these Jewish men were made to sweep the market square in front of their Polish neighbors. At one point here, they were ordered to stop working, were lined up and posed in front of a half dozen German army trucks for a photo. Note the armed German soldiers and SS officers standing behind them. (Photo in the public domain taken by an unnamed Wehrmacht soldier.)

Close-up of previous photo: one SS officer towards the left [widest arrow] and several armed German soldiers posed behind Wieliczka Jews; soldiers grinning for the camera. (Photo in the public domain taken by an unnamed Wehrmacht soldier.)

Another Wehrmacht round-up of Wieliczka Jewish men outside of Rynek Górny 4 on a date between September 7-11, 1939; under German orders, Jewish men made to sweep the upper market square and pick up horse dung with bare hands and buckets; photo taken by unnamed Wehrmacht soldier. (Courtesy Tomasz Wisniewski, Ph.D., Wisniewski Coll. www.bagnowka.pl.)

A Wehrmacht soldier cutting *peiyot*, or religious sidecurls, off the temples of a Wieliczka Jewish man in front of either Rynek Górny 4, 5 or 6 in the upper market square between September 7-11, 1939. (Courtesy Tomasz Wisniewski, Ph.D., Wisniewski Coll. www.bagnowka.pl.)

During these five days, the Wehrmacht cut off Jewish men's sidecurls, or, *peiyot* (phonetic, "pay-yot," or, sidecurls growing long from both temples of a man's head). In one of the first incidents in the upper market square, German soldiers posed more than 43 Jewish men outside of the market's famous buildings, Rynek Górny 4, 5 and 6. Smiling and armed behind them, some soldiers sat in their army trucks while other Wehrmacht posed behind Wieliczka's Jewish men. Nathan, just nine years old, witnessed these events over the five days unsure what lie ahead. He was thankful, however, that his father, Joseph, had not been part of any of these five days' round-ups. Then, everything changed on September 12th, the day on which a Waffen Schutzstaffel company, the armed branch of the Nazi Party's Schutzstaffel organization, or "SS," entered Weiliczka for the first time. Approximately 150 armed men from the SS contingent arrived in their own trucks along and came with additional lorries. Nathan saw about a dozen German soldiers wearing the all-black collared uniforms adorned with the "death's head" skull insignias (worn by the Nazi SS-Totenkopfverbände death units). Nathan was worried about the SS's presence as was Gustava because this contingent acted with a cold and direct callousness. Most of the Germans soldiers in Wieliczka were wearing green uniforms, but now the SS was on the scene and the atmosphere changed. Nathan and his mother saw the ominous skull insignias on the SS soldiers' uniform collars but knew not what they meant. Something was different on September 12th, but what exactly the Jews could never have predicted.

Although the world did not know it at this time, the SS had been specifically tasked by the Third Reich in 1941 with the genocidal killing of an estimated 5.5 to 6 million Jews and five million non-Jewish victims.[2]

But on this particular day, September 12, 1939, the Nazis were in Wieliczka to round up and murder Jews using the same market square as the launching point. With the help the local Polish municipality that created a list of Jewish men to round up and the Poremba's own neighbors, the SS sought to use the square as cover for what may have seemed like just another humiliation / clean up scenario.

Word spread quickly around town that the SS was looking for all Jewish males for forced labor. The SS was working from a list of prominent

---

2. Evans, *The Third Reich at War*, 318.

Observant Wieliczka Jews forced to sweep the upper city square on September 12, 1939 as the Germans supervised to the amusement of their non-Jewish neighbors. Note the soldiers forcibly bringing another Jew to the square in upper right corner. This is the same square Joseph Poremba was brought moments or hours later before 32 Jewish men were put on lorries, driven to a nearby forest and shot by the Germans; photo taken by unnamed Wehrmacht soldier on September 12, 1939. (Courtesy Tomasz Wisniewski, Ph.D., Wisniewski Coll. www.bagnowka. pl; and http://www.belzec.eu/media/files/pages/278/wieliczka_ang.pdf.)

Wieliczka Jews. Unbeknown to the Jews of Wieliczka, finalizing the list was not going to take long because it had mostly been compiled before the Nazis ever arrived in the City. How was this possible a foreign invader could have compiled a list of Jews to round up so quickly? The Nazis must have had advanced help. Did they have an insider?

Working with the SS company commander in Wieliczka was a Pole whose last name was "Mazurowski." He was a municipality clerk for the city before the war who worked as a messenger, but who was later secretly recruited into the German secret service. The local Jews recognized him despite hiding behind the SS uniforms. They knew he worked as a city messenger and after that as a municipal clerk. But on September 12, 1939, he was shockingly working with the SS and pointing at a list on a clipboard. Working undercover the entire time, Mazurowski had been a collaborator in the German secret service for some time. He was the one who complied the list of local Jews to round up. Mazurowski did this with the help of other Wieliczka Poles. The list was put together by Mazurowski and other Poles before the Germans arrived in Wieliczka. The people saw Mazurowski access the list and direct the Germans to the whereabouts of the Jews on this list.[3] With the list in its hands, the SS proceeded to raid Jewish homes looking for specific adult males.

More than a dozen Jewish men heard about the incoming round-up. They immediately abandoned their homes and their families and escaped to the nearby dense forests which surrounded Wieliczka.

Gustava hurried home from the tavern that day and told Joseph what was going on. She told him German troops were fanning out across the city looking for Jewish men. This work assignment was not for cleaning streets in the city square but reportedly for labor outside the city.

She begged him to leave the house and hide in the forests as others had done. "I'm not afraid," he said to Gustava. He calmly turned away, unmoved by all the commotion. He went to an adjacent room in their home, laid down, and took a nap. So many Jewish males had previously fled to Kraków days ago. Others hid in the forests. Very few stayed behind to protect their home and families. But Joseph stayed. He never ran out of fear before and was not convinced that he should react to the pressure building in Wieliczka on this day.

THE NAZI AND POLISH ROUND-UP OF WIELICZKA'S JEWS, SEPTEMBER 12, 1939

That day a crowd of excited Polish teens gathered in the town square where the Germans parked their vehicles. Nathan saw that some of the Polish onlookers appeared interested in seeing the soldiers up-close and personal. But he saw that other Poles came out to the square because they were curious which Jews were on the list for rounding up. He heard them guessing at which Jews were on the list.

After the SS's arrival, Mazurowski remained in the town's main square. The SS then ordered the German troops to fan out throughout town and to locate the Jewish men on the list.

---

3. Meiri, *The Jewish Community of Wieliczka*, 36.

To speed up the process, the Germans handed out chocolate and other candies to the Polish teenagers willing to help them. The eager Poles pointed out known Jewish homes to the German soldiers. Nathan saw adult Polish Christian men accompanying the troops and saw them verify street directions for them. The Nazis wanted to expedite the operation and not waste time deciphering maps and unfamiliar street names. To keep the Polish group with them, the Germans continued to hand out more candy.

Most Polish adults who assisted the Nazi round-up did so without being asked to participate. They were not in it for German candy like the teenagers were. Instead, Nathan watched people he knew actively help the Nazis round up Jews.

A few houses down from Nathan's home lived an 18- or 19-year-old Polish boy. Nathan saw him lead one soldier toward the gate of the Poremba home along with two more Polish teenagers, all of whom Nathan knew. The Polish teens all pointed to the Poremba home and confirmed to the soldier that Joseph Poremba, a name on the list, lived right there at Reymonta #8.

The soldier approached the home alone and knocked. Gustava answered the door, and he walked in, his rifle pointing to the ground. He looked around, but he did not locate Joseph. He then left the residence. He did not speak a word to any of the five Poremba children or to Gustava.

But as the soldier departed empty-handed, all three Polish teens motioned to him to go back inside. One of them yelled "*żyje tam Żyd!*" ("a Jew lives there!"), followed by "*on jest w domu!*" ("he's home!"). The same Polish teen then yelled in German, "*Jude! Jude! Jude!*" and grabbed the soldier by the arm to punctuate the moment. Nathan did not know whether the Nazi understood Polish, but the soldier certainly appeared to clearly understand "*Jude!*". The teens communicated enough information to the soldier such that he went back to the Poremba home and conducted another search. No additional chocolate or candy was given to the three Polish teens that stood watching from the gate. No additional incentive was furnished to prompt them to implore the German to turn his attention back to the Poremba's home. Instead, the trio took great satisfaction in aiding him as Nathan watched their reactions.

Nazi round-ups of Jews typically ended with their placement on a lorry and being driven to an unknown destination. In this photo, a member of the German police kicks a Jew who is climbing onto the back of a truck in Kraków during a round-up for forced labor. Two other Germans look on with derision. (United States Holocaust Memorial Museum, Photo Archives #73174, courtesy of Instytut Pamieci Narodowej.)

Fresh off being prompted again by the three Polish neighbors, the newly determined soldier returned to the Poremba home a second time. Encouraged by the Polish neighbors to back and look again, the soldier returned more resolute. Upon entry this time, he went room-to-room more thoroughly, moving furniture, kicking over a hat and coat rack, and tossing kitchen utensils around in a display of power. It did not take long, and this time he found Joseph laying on a sofa in a room off to the side of the kitchen.

The soldier grabbed Joseph by the arm and woke him up. He shouted at him to stand up and head to the front door of the house. The soldier walked Joseph to the door when Gustava said in German, "*Lass meinen Mann in Ruhe. Wir haben fünf Kinder*" ("Leave my husband alone. We have five children"). The soldier calmly responded, "*Mach dir keine Sorgen, Frau, dein Mann wird heute Abend zu Hause sein*" ("Don't worry woman, your husband will be home this evening").

Joseph was then walked out of his home without a coat or hat. Since Gustava (temporarily) believed her husband would be returned to her by night, she thought he might need a coat. The soldier permitted Gustava to pick up Joseph's coat and hat and give it to him.

Nathan walked outside behind the soldier and his father. As soon as Joseph reached the gate, other soldiers ordered him to put his hands up as they trained their machine guns on him. The three Polish teens congratulated themselves and glared at Nathan as if to say, "What are you going to do about it?" or "Look at what we did to your family."

As the soldiers walked Joseph to the town square, Nathan followed closely behind, as did the three Polish teens. It was as if the Polish teens wanted to see how it might all play out.

When Joseph entered the town square, Nathan witnessed the soldiers beating the Jewish men who had already been rounded up, pistol-whipping, kicking, and punching them. A crowd stood by and watched. Some mocked the Jewish men. Some cheered at the ongoing torture perpetrated by the soldiers. Most smiled as if relieved it was the Jews that were rounded up and beat.

Over the next hour, thirty-two Jewish men were located, brought to the town square one-by-one, and lined up. Then, the SS ordered the thirty-two Jewish men onto the empty lorries, ready to take them away.

Nathan stood watching, bearing witness to one of the first Nazi atrocities committed in Wieliczka. One soldier announced to the crowd that the men would be taken out of city limits to work. However, the destination and nature of the work were not shared. Nathan felt something was not right and did not trust the brief announcement about work outside the city. Neither did the Jewish onlookers who looked on in confusion and desperation.

Nathan saw fear on the faces of the Jewish men on the lorries and on the faces of their families and friends who looked on. Conversely, he saw an unambiguous measure of satisfaction in the faces of most of the Polish onlookers, especially the three Polish teens who were responsible for the Germans locating Joseph.

At one point, the Jewish wife of a man put on a lorry shouted at him for a set of keys for their business. Earlier in the day, the SS looted

Jewish-owned businesses, including Gustava's tavern. The woman wanted to inspect the damage to their own business. The husband on the lorry responded in Yiddish that he was afraid to reach into his pocket and throw her the keys. As the two trucks' engines started up, Joseph told the man in Yiddish to hand him his keys, and he would toss them to his wife. The man beckoned to Joseph to reach into his pocket and retrieve them, and so in this moment of despair, Joseph helped his fellow Jew in need.

Consistent with the man that he was, Joseph never hesitated to come to the aid of a fellow Jew, especially in the face of antisemitism. The man let Joseph reach into his pocket. He took the keys out of the man's pocket, wadded them up, and tossed them to the man's wife. She caught them, and no one seemed to notice. Nathan saw this act gave some comfort to the panicked woman.

Nathan watched. He took notes. He internalized all of it.

There was not much of a challenge for Mazurowski, a Pole working as a Nazi spy, to compile a list of "wanted" Jews. Afterall, he worked for the city and knew who Wieliczka's Jews were. Wieliczka practically rolled out the red carpet and rushed to the assistance of the SS. The SS seemed to think it needed a spy's assistance in compiling a list of Jews, but it turned out the Germans only needed to have involved local Poles to help them point out where Jews were located.

Polish participation in the round-ups of Jews was common, including by Polish police. The Polish police prized catching Jews and running to their German occupiers to show what they found.[4] The local police had home-field advantage and intimate knowledge of the areas the Nazis wanted to search, and where to locate Jews they knew. The Polish police also had a dense network of available informers that pre-dated the German invasion. It became quite easy for the police to help the Nazis locate and round up Polish Jews.[5]

An entire mechanism was set up to hunt for Poland's Jews, set up by the Nazis, and operated under German supervision and control. But everyone on the ground doing the digging and aiding with directions were Poles. Villagers, city-folk, and many a neighbor conducted night

---

4. Jan Grabowski, *Hunt for the Jews* (Indiana University Press, 2013), 101–120.
5. Ibid., 103–104.

watches and reported on suspicions and named names. Local informers under cover of being food market workers, physicians, and farmers reported information up the chain: Polish police, fireman, and others.[6] Together, many Poles comprised a collaboration web that made it nearly impossible for a Jew to hide in Nazi-occupied Poland. So it should have come as no surprise Joseph Poremba's name would be on the Nazi round-up list of Jews set for September 12, 1939. Of course, he would be on the list because he was a Lion of Judah.

By reputation and deed, the city's inhabitants were aware of the many times Joseph Poremba stood up to and acted against local antisemitism. The Germans were intent on eliminating anyone who might lead resistance to their occupation.

What Joseph represented to the Germans was of paramount importance to maintaining a compliant populace under German occupation. The German round-up sought to better the odds and to eliminate influential Jews. Joseph's actions over the decades did not go unnoticed, and his name made its way onto the list. By reputation alone, he was a man the Nazis targeted because local intelligence knew his value to any future resistance movement.

Joseph chose not to run to Kraków when the Germans arrived in Wieliczka. He had chosen not to hide in the forests. He chose to stay and protect his family.

THE MURDER OF THE THIRTY-TWO

The SS trucks finally moved out. After they headed to a nearby forest, Taszyce, Nathan, just nine years old, became more and more concerned as time passed. He was still a child and not yet able to connect all the dots of hearing Hitler's antisemitic speeches in 1938 on a neighbor's radio to the subsequent Nazi invasion on September 1st and to the September 12th round-up of Wieliczka's Jewish males.

---

6. Ofer Aderet, 'Orgy of Murder': The Poles Who 'Hunted" Jews and Turned Them Over to The Nazis, https://www.haaretz.com/world-news/.premium.MAGAZINE-orgy-of-murder-the-poles-who-hunted-jews -and-turned-them-in-1.5430977 (Haaretz.com, 2017).

But Nathan went about playing with his friends in the town square as he waited for his father's return. After all, the soldier told Gustava that Joseph would be home by evening.

One fifteen-year-old Jewish boy, named J. Kornhauser, chose instead to follow the lorries. His father, Leibish Kornhauser, was in one of the lorries. The SS drove the thirty-two Jewish men about three miles to the outskirts of Wieliczka to the forest. There the SS lined the men up in eight rows, four men per row.[7] They were then machine-gunned down, row-by-row, in cold blood in their clothes. There was no "work detail" on this day—only genocide.

Because the Nazis were in a hurry to commit the same atrocity in nearby Limanova, they left the thirty-two corpses where they fell, unburied. J. Kornhauser made it on foot to the scene of the genocide shortly after that and was the first person from Wieliczka to see the outcome. He ran back to town, horrified at what he had seen. Word quickly spread about what happened to the thirty-two men.

After the Holocaust, witnesses' accounts explained that from the appearance of the bullet wounds on the bodies of some of the men, it appeared they had resisted their murderers.[8]

The names of the thirty-two Jewish victims of Wieliczka on September 12, 1939:

Orbach and his son
Armer, Jacob and his son Joseph
Buchstahl, Samuel; Hendler's son-in-law
Bajor, Samuel; Hendler's son-in-law
Blumenfeld, Shmelke and his son Hershel
Goldberg, Abraham, and his son Moshe
Gerber, Isaac; Blumenfeld's son-in-law
Gross, Jacob and his son Samuel
Dancig, Samuel
Hendler, Pinhas and his son Abraham
Heler, Abraham

---

7. Meiri, *The Jewish Community of Wieliczka*, 36.
8. Ibid., 37.

Waldman, Jacob Hirsh, and his son Naphtali
Wishnicki
Winer, Moshe
Melcer, Abraham
Poremba, Joseph
Falk, Meir, and his son Joseph
Fiszer, Moshe
Kornhauser, Leibish
Kriger, Aron
Kaner, Moshe Jacob
Stern and his son

And one more martyr whose name was not remembered by any of the city's Holocaust survivors.[9]

Only Jewish women and children remained to bury the dead. Between the Jewish men who had fled to Kraków or nearby forests between September 1st and September 12th and the thirty-two men just slaughtered, there were no Jewish adult males left in Wieliczka. If any remaining Jewish men returned from hiding, they were understandably too afraid to participate in the burial.

There was no time for grief. Gustava rented a horse and buggy and headed out to the forest with Nathan's eldest sister, Tala, to retrieve Joseph's bullet-torn body. They located Joseph's body among the piles of strewn men and put it on the buggy's platform. They had room for two more bodies, so they took the two adjacent bodies and put them on the wooden platform just the same. They then traveled back to town without saying a word.

When they returned, Nathan got his first look. His father's body had four or five bullet wounds to the chest and one to the head. It is possible it took a subsequent shot to the head to kill Joseph, but equally possible, he decided to turn and face his tormentors and charged at them. Joseph's bullet entry wounds were from the front of his body to his back, perhaps evidence he, in fact, did turn and run towards his killers.

9. Ibid., 37–38.

The only items retrieved from Joseph's body were his pocket watch, wedding ring, and wallet. Tala removed the items and handed them to her mother.

Gustava was heartbroken, inconsolable. War had come, left her a widow, and devasted a family inside of twelve short days. Left with five children, her tavern vandalized and looted, Germans now occupying the country and their town, death, and struggle were all around her. There was also no way to earn a living. Jews were subject to new Nazi law and were immediately banned from their own businesses. Children could no longer attend school, and synagogues were closed.

But they were still alive.

In the span of a few hours, Nathan ceased being a child. When the thirty-two Jewish bodies were prepared for burial, a mass grave in the nearby Jewish cemetery was prepared. Nathan knew his life would never be the same. Darkness had fallen around him.

BURYING THE MARTYRS ON ROSH HASHANA

There was not enough manpower to dig thirty-two individual graves. Never had there been a need to bury so many people at one time in Wieliczka. The families then decided to either dig one mass grave or two large graves that could fit sixteen bodies in each. There was no other way to remedy the lack of available manpower.

The Poles in town refused to help the Jews dig graves. Some might have been willing to help but were afraid to do so. Others were glad Jews had been killed. It was not German candy that motivated some to help them in the round-up. It was their antisemitism.

By then, it was midnight, and on September 13, 1939, Erev Rosh Hashanah (the Jewish New Year). Instead of preparing for *yontif* (the beginning of a Jewish holiday), Wieliczka's Jews were instead busy burying their dead.

Without sufficient help, it was decided two plots to hold sixteen bodies each was not possible due to lack of assistance. It was determined more shallow plots would be prepared, big enough to store three to five bodies per plot. Some families did not have the money to afford a burial. A few

Former Sonderkommando, Nathan Poremba's cousin, Yossek Bakalarz, and his wife, Helen, at one of the crematoriums at Auschwitz-Birkenau, August 29, 1995, a trip that also took them to Wieliczka where he verified the monument to the Thirty-Two Martyrs was removed by Christian Poles after the war. (Courtesy Tova Shemer.)

Jewish families that had not lost a father pitched in to help. Gustava was in no position to help but did so anyways and put the extra money to cover the burials for two families with no money. She informed these women that their husbands' bodies would be placed in the same grave as Joseph.

There were no plans to erect headstones lest the Germans knock them down. Simple metal name plates were placed on the sides of the large area where the thirty-two men were laid to rest.

No one could say *kaddish* (the mourner's prayer) in the Poremba's shul because the Germans had destroyed it. They desecrated and turned it into a horse stable. They ripped out of each row of pews, destroyed the Torah scrolls and ark that housed them, and leveled the *bimah* (the raised platform with reading desks where the rabbi and cantor sit facing the congregation).

By the end of this horrible day, Nathan vowed he would somehow avenge his father. He knew the ringleader of the three Polish teens who pointed out the Poremba home. He knew who the other two boys were as well. He knew that, but for their actions, Joseph might have escaped the round-up. Maybe then he would have fled to Kraków and lived. Or run away to the surrounding forests.

Nathan had no idea when he could take revenge, but he promised himself to remember the boys' names and when the time and place was right to reckon with them.

ERASING WIELICZKA'S GENOCIDE

After the Holocaust, a stone monument was erected in Wieliczka, where the thirty-two men had been laid to rest. The monument listed their names, memorialized, and documented the Nazi round-up and the subsequent murders. Later, in the 1970s or early 1980s, the local Poles removed and destroyed the monument in the act of blatant antisemitism.[10] The name plates that were put up on the sides of the graves were also removed. None of this was undertaken or directed by Soviet officials.

Post-war scrubbing of Poland's complicit history is no mirage. Wieliczka's Christian Poles sought to whitewash what they had done to voluntarily assist in the German round-up of its Jews on September 12, 1939. Elimination of evidence or discussion about the incident was paramount not only to Poland but to Wieliczka by way of the monument's destruction. Snuffing out the fact Jews once lived in Wieliczka goes hand in hand with trying to erase the city's and its citizens' participation with the Nazis on that fateful day.

Antisemitism in Wieliczka took to a new form on September 12, 1939, and saw Poles eagerly assist Nazis in rounding up Jews. Decades later, the next generation of Poles saw to it to desecrate the graves by removing both the monument along with the name plates. There were no Nazis around to impress, or work with, just Poles. Deleting the memory

---

10. Józef ("Yossek") Bakalarz, Nathan Poremba's first cousin and an Auschwitz sonderkommando survivor, visited Wieliczka in 1995, verified the monument and name plates memorializing the thirty-two Jewish men murdered on September 12, 1939 had been removed after the Holocaust by resident Wieliczka Poles, not by Soviet officials.

Nazis routinely rounded up observant Jews, shaved their beards, and cut their peiyot.
(Courtesy Alamy: https://www.alamy.com.)

of the dead is to kill them a second time. But emphasizing this ugly occurrence stands in defiance to Poland's curious denials it was complicit in the Holocaust. Poland's efforts to erase its complicity with the Nazis are undone by clumsy attempts to whitewash its own history.

One could argue that Wieliczka's Poles only helped the Nazis with their round-up because they were told the Jews were being sent on a work detail. Maybe they believed what the Nazis said. But the destruction of the monument is likely evidence of a people eager to erase its complicity with the Nazis. Moreover, knocking down and removing the monument to those that were murdered says much about feelings towards Wieliczka's Jewish history to give credence to the argument Christian Poles thought the round-up was merely for work detail. Why the overreaction if Poles had nothing to do with the round-up?

To date, the monument to Wieliczka's Jews murdered on September 12, 1939 remains destroyed and the mass grave unmarked.

Modern Poland has endeavored to foist an unsupportable public relations campaign insisting it was not an accomplice to the Holocaust. But its unambiguous conduct during the Holocaust in Wieliczka at the government and civilian levels shows otherwise. The curious post-war removal of the monument is evidence of Polish participation with the Nazis on both levels as it concerns Wieliczka.

FURTHER POLISH COMPLICITY IN WIELICZKA, 1939–1942

Polish abuse of Jews and other criminal conduct took on a different look later in 1939. After the thirty-two Jewish men were murdered, city officials demanded 8,000 zlotys (phonetic, "z-lot-tees," Poland's monetary unit) in new taxes from Wieliczka's Jews. The Poles exploited fear among the Jews by imposing this new tax and threatened imprisonment or death if it was not paid.[11] Then, at the end of 1941, Wieliczka officials continued their tax-exploitation schemes of the remaining Jewish residents. The new mayor, Rosig, declared that the municipal bathhouse suddenly needed restoration, and if the Jews contributed tens of thousands of zloty, he would protect them from the Germans. If Wieliczka Jews fell short on cash Rosig declared, he would take remuneration in jewelry. Finally, in July 1942, officials determined to implement a tax of 500,000 zlotys on Wieliczka's Jews, knowing deportation orders were arriving in less than a month.[12] The Polish authorities might as well extort Wieliczka's Jews for what they could while they were still alive.

Just nine days later, on Yom Kippur eve, two German soldiers harassed an elderly Wieliczka Jew walking quietly on the street. They ordered him to stand against a wall and tore his *tzitzit* (phonetic, "tsi-seet," or a knotted and fringed religious garment worn under a shirt by a Jewish male) from his upper body. One soldier placed it through the bayonet of the other's rifle, tearing it further, and as it hung there in tattered pieces, the other soldier burned it. A crowd of more than twenty Poles gathered and cheered the German soldiers on. Then one of the soldiers took out a pair of scissors and

---

11. Megargee, *USHMM Encyclopedia of Camps and Ghettos*, vol. 2, 591–592.
12. Meiri, *The Jewish Community of Wieliczka*, 40.

cut off the Jewish man's *peiyot* and shortened his long beard. In so doing, they cut the lobe of one of his ears off. As the bystander Poles laughed and watched, the old man stood there shivering in fear, standing tight to the wall with blood dripping from his ear onto his clothes.[13]

At least one Wieliczka Jew witnessed this incident from afar. Word then spread throughout the Jewish community about the German attack on an orthodox Jew enthusiastically watched by the Poles.

Nathan learned of the Yom Kippur eve attack from a neighbor. Fresh off watching Poles turn in his father only days earlier, he was told about the Poles who cheered on the Nazi assault of an observant Jew.

It is a shameful lie to claim Poles did not participate with the Germans in assaults of Jews. It is true Poles assisted in the round-ups of the Polish Jews. It equally true Polish police and city officials participated with the Nazis in locating Jews. Whether for money, candy, or, sport Poles were very much part of the Nazi killing machine, serving in various roles they willingly volunteered to undertake.

---

13. Ibid., 47.

CHAPTER FIVE

A WOMAN OF VALOR: A MOTHER'S SACRIFICE TO SAVE HER CHILDREN

REFUSAL TO WEAR THE STAR OF DAVID ARMBAND

For the next six months, from September 13, 1939, to March 1940, no German troops appeared in Wieliczka. Instead, they had moved out and headed East and Southeast. In their wake instead left behind new regulations and restrictions for Polish Jews, enforced by the Polish police and Wieliczka city officials. Cheders and synagogues were closed. Jews were prohibited from going to school. Jews were not permitted to travel or own businesses. Wieliczka Jews were on notice that a violation of any of these laws was punishable with local incarceration, deportation to an unknown location (labor or concentration camp), or summary execution. The only activity Jews were permitted was cleaning public streets upon order of the local Polish police.

During this period, Wieliczka, like all of Poland, required Jewish men to "register for work," which entailed either public works projects or slave labor for the Nazis. Nathan knew Wieliczka Jews were ordered to travel each day to construct the nearby Kraków labor camp, named Płaszów. However, Wieliczka Jews had no idea what they were building at the time or its purpose. In time people learned that Płaszów was constructed to be a labor camp to house Jews near Kraków.

Meanwhile, Wieliczka Jews fled a handful at a time every few days. It was relatively quiet in Wieliczka at this time, but rumors continually circulated about deportations and executions of Jews. Sometimes, a Polish policeman in Wieliczka would beat a Jew to death or raid a Jewish home and take a person away, never to be seen again. There was rarely legal cause for this torment other than the "crime" of being Jewish coupled with a sadistic police force. At this time, there were no Nazi operations in Wieliczka, no lorries rolling into town for round-ups of Jews, no troops stationed on the ground, and no SS officers present.

But the rumors about deportation and murder deeply affected Nathan. There was insecurity, fear, and worry without end. Most of the rumors could not be corroborated. "Did you hear they raided Moshe's home and took him away?" was always table talk. Conversely, things were significantly worse for Jews in nearby Kraków, where the Nazis did maintain a heavy military and Gestapo presence. As a result, Kraków Jews began to flee south to Wieliczka, which created terrible overcrowding.

In November 1939, Polish Jews age ten and older were also required to identify themselves by wearing a white band on their arms with the Star of David in the center. The German military and civilian authorities imposed this. The governor-general of Nazi-occupied Poland, Hans Frank, issued the order. Nathan was nearing ten years of age and did not want to be stopped and questioned about his age or why he was not wearing the Star, being close to ten. His mother encouraged him to wear it now, at age nine and a half, but he had other ideas. He refused to wear the armband and told Gustava he would not wear it two months short of his tenth birthday or after his birthday. He could not understand why he should advertise what he was, only to be easily targeted and harassed by the Polish police or his Polish neighbors, let alone German soldiers.

Then Nathan had an idea. At nine years of age, he surmised that due to the recent overcrowding of people in Wieliczka coming from Kraków, he could hide among the greater number of people on the streets. The idea of not wearing the armband gave him a sense of relative freedom of movement. He saw an opportunity. He could potentially blend in and sneak around town as a small boy undetected on crowded streets without wearing a Star of David armband in order to pose as a non-Jew. To avoid detection by his immediate neighbors seeing him out in public without the armband, he would sneak out of the back of the house and proceed through an alleyway for a few blocks before reappearing on busy streets.

But Gustava insisted he wear the armband. She saw in her son a restless, non-compliant little boy. She thought it a dangerous rebellious phase. But Nathan explained to his mother that he noticed the police did not harass or detain Christian kids whose misconduct might warrant detention or citation. It appeared the armband made Jews the only target for the local police. This reinforced Nathan's belief that if he did not wear the armband, he would be safer. He assumed it would enable him to walk around like anyone else without the fear of being stopped. The influx of Jews fleeing Kraków created so much new foot traffic that it provided him cover to get around unnoticed. He explained his reasoning to Gustava, but after losing her husband, she was in no mood to debate her young son on potential life or death issues. Nathan did not agree. He argued that not wearing the armband made him safer and might let him freely shop for food for the family. Always thinking, always debating, and adapting, he won his mother over.

Nathan was testing his boundaries. Not wearing the armband was a possible way to leave town without being stopped. He counted on Wieliczka Poles and police focusing their attention on the newly arriving Jews, not on him. Why abide by a rule that brought attention to oneself, restricted freedom, and threatened his well-being?

He explained all of this to his mother. She argued with him, but she could not seem to convince him to lay low and wear the armband.

"My blue eyes will save me. You will see," he told Gustava. Nathan reasoned that with light brown, almost dark blonde hair, fair skin, and blue eyes, he just might fit in as a Pole. Add to that, he figured, not wearing a Star of David armband, in a crowded town, he could get around without anyone noticing him.

From late 1939 through early 1940, Polish officials often knocked on the Poremba door to take Nathan to mandatory work. In October 1939, the official Nazi policy was labor for Jewish adult males, enforced by the local Polish police. Gustava would answer the door, and she would simply say her son was nine years old and too small to work. Usually,

One of several Star of David Armbands the Nazis required Polish
Jews to wear in 1939–1940. (Courtesy National Holocaust Centre &
Museum, United Kingdom.)

the person left without further questioning, but sometimes the official
would still demand Nathan present himself. Always within earshot of
these conversations, Nathan would slip out through a back window of
the house, ready to run. He would hear the knock on the door, hide in
the house, listen to the conversation at the door, assess the threat level,
and sneak out of the house if he had to. This cat and mouse routine went
on for almost ten months.

Without the armband, Nathan could patronize Polish food markets
and sundry stores where he bought food for the family. Jews were not
permitted in Polish markets, and with Jewish-owned ones closed, food
was scarce, opportunities few and far between. His three older sisters had
temporarily found jobs for pay as maids in Polish homes. But no armband
meant more freedom of movement for him. He became the designated
shopper and food provider for the family, a job he volunteered for and
carried out without a hitch. In the early going of this resistance, there was
not one instance where a neighbor recognized Nathan.

But one day, this freedom to move around nearly cost Nathan his
life. He walked into a Polish food store on the outskirts of Wieliczka,
looking to buy flour, cooking oil, and other items. Suddenly he saw the
very teenager who sent the German soldier back into the Poremba home
on September 12, 1939 to look for his father. Nathan was smart enough
not to react abruptly, not to run out in fear, and not to say anything to

A group of Jewish men wearing the compulsory Star of David armbands in Kraków while made to shovel coal off the back of a truck between 1940–1941. (United States Holocaust Memorial Museum, courtesy Archiwum Panstwowe w Krakowie, Photo Archives #73208.)

prompt an incident. There was no way to take revenge all alone, not in a store full of Poles. Besides, he was breaking the law shopping, and the teen knew Nathan was Jewish, so yelling something was out of the question. Just as bad, Nathan was out in public without the armband. The Poles in the store would likely have reported him to the police if he caused an incident.

Instead, Nathan kept calm. He shopped and pretended he did not see the teen and was careful not to be seen by him. Any revenge would have to wait. But a few moments later, the Polish teen caught sight of Nathan. He did a double-take on Nathan, and their eyes met for a split second. Nathan was certain the young man recognized him, so he quickly paid and hurried out of the busy store before anything developed. As he slowly made his way calmly out of the store, he heard nothing to signal that there would be any pursuit. A few feet outside, he braced for the worst, ready to run, but nothing. The teen likely did not recognize Nathan, but Nathan could not wrap his head around the fact he had not. They were neighbors, after all. Had this escalated, Nathan would assuredly have been pursued by authorities for violating the armband law. But for whatever reason, nothing ensued.

On the way home, Nathan kept an eye over his shoulder, but there was no chase. He had escaped a potentially explosive situation. Nathan chose not to tell his mother or sisters about running into the teenager. He would only worry Gustava and lead to her revoke permission. He kept the incident a secret.

HIDING IN NEARBY MIECHÓW

By late 1941, Wieliczka's Jews were required to stay within the city's limits. If anyone challenged the order, he or she would be shot on the spot.[1] The noose on Wieliczka's Jews was tightening. Any attempt to escape the city attached with it the steepest of prices.

By early 1942, things changed for the worse for Wieliczka's Jewish population. Unknown to Polish Jews, on January 20, 1942, the Wannsee Conference was held outside of Berlin. It was here the Nazis decided to terminate the current policy of genocide-by-bullets, and in its place, institute a more expeditious format of killing Europe's Jews, a new method of killing that took a lesser psychological toll on the perpetrators. The Conference codified many things, but utmost for the Reich, it made mass genocide official policy. The Nazis would now utilize extermination camps. As a result, over the next twelve months, 1.7 million Jews were murdered by the Nazis. In 1942, more and more Wieliczka Jews were taken away and never seen again. The rumors of the previous year's slowly became first-hand knowledge and impossible to ignore. Still, some still Jews refused to believe it.

After various deportations from the Kraków Ghetto in June 1942, Wieliczka's Jews became much more concerned about their own fate. Their rabbis urged the community to endure German brutalities with submissiveness, repeating: "Let the beast devour."[2] These stories frightened Nathan, now twelve years old. He became as restless as he was helpless, which led him to do the unthinkable.

He asked his mother if he could run away. Alone. Immediately.

---

1. Megargee, *USHMM Encyclopedia of Camps and Ghettos*, vol. 2, 592.
2. Ibid.

Gustava worried about her only son, her youngest child. He was still too young and slight of build to do a man's job, to do forced labor and survive it. He was too young to find a domestic job as his sisters had. She knew he still refused to wear the Star of David armband and liked to sneak out of the house and not come back for hours. She could not find "a place" for him to settle, but one thing was clear to her: her son felt caged and wanted out of Wieliczka. To him, the town felt like a ticking time-bomb.

She made the gut-wrenching decision to allow him to leave at the same time, hoping to maximize the odds he might survive. But, now that the disappearance of so many Jews was becoming fact, she chose

Miechów: twenty-five miles northeast of Kraków.

to give in to Nathan's new bold idea. After much thought, she agreed to send him to Miechów to Gita, Joseph's sister. Gita agreed to hide Nathan and his youngest sister, Fela, in a Christian home near Gita's house. Little did they both know this was a dress rehearsal for a much tougher decision yet to come. But for now, this might prevent Nathan from doing something rash.

It was April or May 1942, and Fela, age fourteen, and Nathan, twelve, set out according to the plan to get to Gita in Miechów. The closest train station in Kraków would be the one to get them to Miechów. Neither of them wore the Star of David armband, and neither carried any luggage lest someone suspect they were escaping town. They purchased tickets and took the train from Kraków to Miechów without incident. Sitting on the train among Christian Poles was no easy task. Trying not to stare, Nathan managed glimpses at people whose clothes were freshly pressed and who had full bellies. He stared at businessmen apparently on their way work, their lives seemingly not turned upside like his own family. No such luxuries existed for Jews. It was difficult to conceal the want, the envy, and hunger, but to survive the train ride without detection, he and his sister had to play their roles flawlessly.

Nathan and Fela shuttled back and forth between the Miechów Ghetto and the Christian lady's home Gita had located for them. It was not their idea, but it was a smart one, albeit temporary. The Christian lady helping them did not want to risk her own family's safety by having two new children suddenly show up at her home. Neighbors could easily spot new arrivals, which might invite unwanted attention. So, she devised a plan for the two kids to go back and forth from her home to the ghetto to reduce any suspicions they were being hidden in her home. This way, they looked more like visitors coming and going and not residents. Creating ambiguity about where the children lived was a safer tact to disguise the fact they were hiding.

Fortunately, as small young children, Nathan and Fela could sneak in and out of the Miechów Ghetto without any trouble. Then, in mid-June, Nathan's older sister, Sala, wrote to her two siblings in Miechów and told them things had once again quieted down in Wieliczka. She begged them

Photo of man standing inside the Miechów Ghetto on July 11, 1941
(Courtesy Geoffrey P. Megargee, *The United States Holocaust Memorial
Museum Encyclopedia of Camps and Ghettos*, vol. 2, 540).

to come back home. The next day Gita gave Nathan and Fela money,
and they once again ventured out, purchased train tickets, and went back
home undetected. When they arrived, the family was so happy to see
them. The five children and their mother were together once again. They
made a promise to each other to stick together and not separate again.

But just one week later, the rumors of deportations and death camps
picked up. But this time, the chatter was quite different. The word was
that mass deportation orders were being posted in small towns by the
Germans and Polish police. The round-ups were becoming more official,
orderly, and supervised by armed Nazis and Polish armed police. These
new orders were directing Jews to leave their homes on a certain date,

show up at an exact time; and, be prepared to board a train to "some" unknown destination. The orders required Jewish elderly, the infirm, women, and children to be rounded up for "resettling." The stories about "Polish ghettos being liquidated" or emptied were becoming rampant. Ghetto liquidation stories coupled with simultaneous deportation orders had a horrible effect on Nathan and his siblings. This was not just another episode of the noose tightening on cities. This seemed to Nathan to be more finite and like "the end." While many adults engaged in wishful thinking, taking the deportation orders literally as a "resettlement" event, Nathan did not. He put no stock in what the Nazis promised. He never forgot the roundup of his father in what was described as "work detail."

He did the unimaginable: he asked his mother if he could run away. Not to run away to Gita's house, not to Gita's Christian neighbor again, either. Just run away. Forever. So that he could live without these rumors over his head.

"I Want To Live"

In July 1942, Nathan approached his mother and said he wanted to leave home and go back to Miechów. He explained he was too afraid to stay in Wieliczka. "I want to live," he told her. "I don't want to die." Gustava was shocked, for they had re-united, and, at least temporarily, things felt a little calmer in Wieliczka.

But Nathan told his mother he wanted to make his way to his Aunt Gita again. He explained he would use this destination as a way point until he figured out his next stop. He could no longer sit trapped in Wieliczka, waiting to die, waiting for deportation orders to be posted.

Gustava could not argue with him. He was not asking permission to go. Rather, he was telling his mother what he wanted to do. He insisted he wanted to leave.

He was too scared to stay in a place he knew to be on the brink of destruction. On the other hand, Gustava knew leaving with five children was not feasible. Moving as a group of six would surely attract attention, with or without the required armbands. But there was no way to quell the fire raging in Nathan's chest, either.

Nathan was engaging in the act of resistance: choosing the unknown, alone without family. Gustava had tears in her eyes. She had little to offer in response. What could she say? She knew what she had to do. Here was one of her children telling her he had to leave because *he wanted to live.* He came to her to ask for her blessing, not so much her permission.

Why would a twelve-year-old boy want to abandon the family home? Why would he want to leave his four sisters and mother? Why did he not want to sit tight in the (temporary) safety provided by his family in their own home?

Nathan had no idea what he would do after arriving in Miechów and seeing Gita. He had no long-term plan. He had no connections, and he had no money or dependable food source. He knew no one who could smuggle him out of Poland even if he had the money. Quite honestly, it was the plan of a boy, the plan of an inexperienced person. But it was resistance because it was an expression of life, a response to German occupation, and restrictive laws. Nathan never considered running away to Soviet-held areas where some Jews fled to. He had extended family in Miechów, and his only instinct was to head in that direction, even if a temporary solution.

Nathan was armed with the only thing he would need: an indescribable will to live. He was haunted by his father being taken away, lined up, and gunned down. Joseph was not worried or afraid on September 12, 1939, but he also did not know what the Nazi machine brought with it. Conversely, Nathan knew, and he refused to sit and wait at home for his executioners.

Broken, Gustava thought only of her son's wishes. She thought not of her own.

Gustava gathered all the money she had and called Fela, the youngest daughter, over. She sat Nathan and Fela down and said, "Here is all the money. You must both leave. Right now, today, this minute."

The two took no clothes, no luggage, nothing but the clothes on their backs. Neither of them wore a Star of David armband, something Nathan encouraged Fela to leave behind.

Gustava said, "Wait." She left the living room where the other three children had gathered. Gustava came back minutes later and handed

Nathan his father's pocket watch. He put it in his pants pocket and said, "This is all I'm taking."

This would be the last time Nathan ever saw his mother and three sisters, Tala, Esta, and Sala. Leaving and walking away from them left a mark on him that lasted his entire life. The reason? He survived the Shoah, and Gustava did not. His three sisters also did not survive.

But the focus of this moment was on a mother's love and maternal duty to preserve her children's lives. In their goodbye and their last moment together, a mother put herself aside and put life into her son and daughter. It was the second gift of life this mother, a valiant woman of valor, gave her two youngest children. Letting them both go meant life, which constituted the toughest decision any parent could be called upon to make.

Gustava was determined to chance fate and remain in the house, as many Jews did, believing deportation orders were nothing more than false or merely about relocation.

Nathan's decision came as no shock to Gustava. She watched him when he would not wear the Star of David. She saw him ignore travel restrictions and openly shop in Polish markets despite the prohibition against Jews doing so. Nathan was too restless to sit and wait to be rounded up and killed as his father had. Nathan felt like he was drowning under these conditions. He wanted to run away. The walls were closing in. Waiting in Wieliczka to see what would happen was not the way Nathan wanted to live. And he reaffirmed to Gustava just that: he wanted to live.

A WOMAN OF VALOR

The significance of motherhood in Judaism takes on a special role. This is evident throughout the Hebrew Bible. King Solomon wrote the poem Eishet Chayil ("Woman of Valor") as part of Proverbs, a book of great wisdom. We sing this ode to women before making Kiddush on Friday evening as Jews welcome in the Shabbat Queen. Among the Hebrew alphabet's elegant curves and contours is a blueprint for a life of meaning, a life of wisdom. *Eishet Chayil* symbolizes such wisdom and foundation.[3]

---

3. Karen Wolfers-Rapaport, Eishet Chayil: A Pictorial View of the Woman of Valor, https://www .chabad.org/theJewishWoman/article_cdo/aid/3270084/jewish/Eishet-Chayil-A-Pictorial-View-of-the -Woman-of-Valor.html (Chabad.org/TheJewishWoman, 2016).

Jewish women are conduits of life and intuition. They nourish, sustain, and generate creation.[4]

Motherhood makes its first appearance on the biblical scene by serving as the source of the first woman's name. As told in Genesis: "The man called his wife's name Eve, (Hava), because she was the mother of all living things" (*em kol chai*). Genesis 3:20. Though the woman's name is integrally associated with motherhood, the name of the first man, Adam, is in no way connected to his serving as the progenitor of humanity. Not like a woman's.[5] For the mother, "the image of the baby, the memory of an infant held in her arms, the picture of herself playing, laughing, embracing, nursing, cleaning, and so forth, never vanishes. She always looks upon her child as upon a baby who needs her help and company, and whom she has to protect and shield."[6]

Another mother might have denied her twelve-year-old boy's request to run away during wartime. But Gustava responded with selfless love and gave Nathan what he requested: the freedom to run. No one could have known what would follow.

Gustava's decision was nothing short of the ultimate act of love by a mother, as only a mother could understand and permit, however painful it was to provide.

Nathan did not say goodbye to Tala, Sala, or Esta. He was scared, and he was in a hurry to leave and did not want to be talked out of his by his sisters, who were so influential in his life. He had secured his mother's decision one-on-one and did not want a subsequent debate with the other children. Gustava said he should go with Fela, and the two immediately left. Before opening the front door, Nathan looked up and back at his mother and leaned into her to give her a short hug. He did not know this was the last goodbye, and he had no way of knowing. To him, it was goodbye until it was safe to return, whenever that may be. It did not have any finality to it as nothing was certain. On the other hand, Gustava's eyes welled up as she fought back the tears. She did not want to

---

4. Ibid.

5. Meir Soloveichik, *The Jewish Mother: A Theology*, originally published in Azure, Spring, 2005.

6. Rabbi Joseph B. Soloveitchik, *Family Redeemed: Essays on Family Relationships* (New York: Toras HaRav Foundation, 2000), 163.

break down in front of her children. She did not want to signal to them that she was unsure of the decision she had made. She was confident in her decision about Nathan and Fela.

Tala pleaded with Nathan, "our father went out that door and never came back, but it was at gunpoint that he left. You are leaving on your own. Why?" Nathan had not the courage to rebut or engage. He could only muster a faint whisper back to her, "I have to run. I want to live." Off he went without dragging the moment out any further.

Woman of Valor, "Eshet Chayil," in classical harp shape adorned with grape vines by Israeli artist, Avraham Goldfarb, Jerusalem, Israel. (Courtesy Avraham Goldfarb.)

Two children, alone, without luggage, set off into an unforgiving world of chaos in wartime Poland. Not exactly a formula for success. Meanwhile, the four left behind could only hope for the best.

WITNESS TO CATTLE CARS HEADED TO AUSCHWITZ, TREBLINKA, AND BEŁŻEC

The two children set out for the train station in hopes of making it to Miechów. Without Star of David armbands adorning their arms, they confidently purchased tickets and took the first train to Kraków. They arrived at their destination without incident and patiently waited at the Kraków station for the train to take them to Miechów. During that wait, they watched four freight trains loaded with people come through the station. They had no idea where these people were coming from or why they were crammed into cattle cars. These trains were not typical passenger trains at all. The passengers seemed to be in distress and suffering. Nathan and Fela heard Yiddish and Hebrew being spoken in the cattle cars. They could also hear Jews praying inside the tightly packed cars.

The two did not react to what they saw as the trains came and went. The two had questions, but they had to stifle them. What they had seen shook them both to their cores. Where were the trains going, and for what purpose? They stayed silent.

The train cars were cramped for space and were without much air circulation. They heard heavy breathing, babies crying, panic, and pleas for food and water. In the summer of 1942, neither Nathan nor Fela understood why people would willingly travel under such conditions. But they quickly realized the trains were holding people against their will.

The first rumors in Poland were that the Germans were sending trains full of Jews to resettle. Another set of rumors were that overpacked trains took Jews to killing centers. It was hard to know what they were looking at. Nathan saw names painted on some of the box cars. He saw the names "Auschwitz," "Treblinka," and "Bełżec" on the cars of three of the four trains they saw. The two children knew Oświęcim was approximately 68 km or 42 miles from Kraków but had no idea what "Treblinka" and "Bełżec" was or where these places were even located. Nathan and Fela had no idea what areas were assigned for the resettlement of the Jews.

Track-side view of the Wielickza train station, as depicted by a photo on a postcard mailed within Poland on January 10, 1904; it is here Nathan purchased train tickets in 1942 while posing as a non-Jew, testing his boundaries, a station from which he travelled to and from Miechów several times. The caption on the postcard reads "new train station." (Photo in the public domain.)

Rear, track side of the Wielickza train station, inoperable and boarded up, taken in approximately 2013. (Photo in the public domain.)

Regardless of the questions they had, Fela and Nathan had to be careful not to react. They could not show worry, fear, or confusion. They were posing as Christian Poles, and so they knew they had to remain in character, indifferent and unmoved by what they saw and heard on these trains.

Nathan felt helpless watching. He asked himself, "was running away increasing or decreasing the odds of survival? Did I make the right decision to leave home? Was it better to be on the run and risk being caught or smarter to stay in town and obey the incoming deportation orders? Maybe they would send us to a safe resettlement region?" He had no way to know the answers to any of these questions.

Gustava, too, asked if she had made the right decision in sending her son and daughter away. Did she increase, or decrease, the chances of their survival? There was no handbook for any of this. There was only a gut instinct to follow.

CHAPTER SIX

THE MURDER OF WIELICZKA'S REMAINING JEWS

BACK TO MIECHÓW

Arriving back in Miechów a second time brought no heroes' welcome. It was back to the previous routine of shuttling between Gita's house and the Miechów Ghetto, the same strategy employed before; to avoid detection and keep on the move and avert suspicion. Nathan and Fela decided to only come to Gita's house at night under cover of darkness and enter through the back of the home. This tactic was to keep neighbors from seeing the same children coming and going daily.

Since this was their second time seeking refuge in the Miechów Ghetto, Nathan and Fela determined to change their routines. Instead of relying on guard shift changes and timing those to enter and leave, they employed new ways to get in and out. One was to sneak in and out with work groups re-entering or leaving the ghetto. While guards were busy screening the papers and permits, the children walked in and out when guards' attention was elsewhere. Nathan and Fela also used the ghetto sewers to get in and out. Lastly, Nathan and Fela snuck through the ghetto perimeter where some of the more abandoned and dilapidated buildings sat with no wires, barricades, or gates around them.

By August 26, 1942, word reached Miechów that a deportation order had been issued by the Nazis and posted by Polish police for Wieliczka's Jews. The two children had very mixed feelings. Yes, they had left home, apparently just in time, but they had left behind their mother and three older sisters in so doing. The children tried not to discuss the guilt they both felt. They acknowledged that had they remained home they would likely be on a train to who knew where. Escape then would have been impossible. They knew leaving home had saved their lives, at least temporarily. But they also felt remorse for having run when their mother and three sisters did not.

DEPORTATION BY THE NAZIS AND POLISH POLICE

On August 27, 1942, Jews from Wieliczka were ordered by the Gestapo and local police to report to the main square. Every little town and village surrounding Wieliczka also ordered Jews to report to their main squares. A heavy Polish police presence joined German troops who formed a perimeter around Wieliczka much larger than anyone had ever seen before. Wieliczka was surrounded by several Nazi units and Polish auxiliary police.[1] No escape would be possible with this blocking of every major and minor road in and out of Wieliczka.

The deportation order imposed on Wieliczka's Jews was signed by the SS Commander of Kraków *and* the Kraków Polish police on August 26, 1942. The order was posted in the town that same day. The Polish police from Kraków had jurisdiction and authority over its sister city to the southeast, Wieliczka, well before the German invasion.

Approximately 700 healthy young Jewish men were selected and determined to be fit for work. They were sent to labor camps at either Płaszów or Stalowa Wola. They were quickly put on lorries and sent away.

Preceding the August 27th round-up was a bit of Nazi trickery. On August 15th, following the order of the newly arrived Gestapo official, Kunde, a modern hospital was established in Wieliczka near the train station. But this was meant to be a trap to fool Wieliczka Jews to congregate in one place to streamline the August 27th deportation.[2] Wieliczka Jews brought one hundred and thirteen sick people to the new hospital.[3] On August 24th, these patients were driven to the Niepołomicka Forest and shot dead in the Kozie Górki woods.[4]

---

1. Megargee, *USHMM Encyclopedia of Camps and Ghettos*, vol. 2, 593.
2. Meiri, *The Jewish Community of Wieliczka*, 41.
3. Spector, *The Encyclopedia of Jewish Life Before and During the Holocaust*, 1442.
4. Ibid.

On August 27th, another seven hundred elderly and physically infirm Jews were put on different lorries headed to a nearby forest in Niepołomicka. Again, they were forced to undress, lined up, and shot in pairs into trenches the Nazis had dug the day before.[5]

This left about 8,000 Jews, all healthy women and children.[6] Approximately 6,000 were ordered to board trains in waves at the station in Wieliczka for Bełżec. Upon arrival, they were immediately killed in the gas chambers.[7] Hundreds more were sent to the forced labor camp in Stalowa Wola and hundreds more to the Płaszów work camp. The remaining people were taken to the Niepołomicka Forest and shot.[8]

SS squads were then led around once again by local Poles, both police and residents. They went street-by-street, neighborhood-by-neighborhood in Wieliczka, looking for any Jews that were hiding. Hundreds of Jews were found this way and executed on the spot.[9]

The initial trains loaded with Wieliczka Jews were sent to Bełżec, a death camp.[10] The SS soon realized it would take too many trains and too much time to transport all 8,000 Jews to Bełżec. So, after they had sent 6,000 to Bełżec, ordered hundreds to the aforementioned labor camps and forest, the SS simply ambushed the remaining Jews at the Wieliczka train station and gunned them all down.

For some months after the massacre of the Wieliczka Jews, the Nazis continued to search the city for surviving Jews. They caught hundreds of more Jews this way. Those, too, were shot on the spot or brought to the Jewish cemetery in Wieliczka and tortured before they were murdered.[11]

Nathan heard all of this while moving between his Aunt Gita's home and the Miechów Ghetto. He felt guilt for having evaded the massacre in Wieliczka, but also gratitude that his bold move had, at least for now, saved his life.

There was no way he could know whether his mother and three sisters had escaped town before it was closed off. There was no way for him

5. Meiri, *The Jewish Community of Wieliczka*, 42.
6. Ibid., 40.
7. Ibid., 43.
8. Spector, *The Encyclopedia of Jewish Life Before and During the Holocaust*, 1442.
9. Meiri, *The Jewish Community of Wieliczka*, 42.
10. Spector, *The Encyclopedia of Jewish Life Before and During the Holocaust*, 1442.
11. Meiri, *The Jewish Community of Wieliczka*, 43.

to confirm whether they had reported to the main square as the deportation order required. He had no way to know if they were sent by train to Bełżec to be gassed, murdered at the train station, sent to a concentration or forced labor camp.

A 2013 photo of the entrance to the Wieliczka train station that Nathan utilized while posing as a Christian Pole to get to and from Miechów and Bochnia in May 1942; and the site from where the Germans rounded-up / sent thousands of Wieliczka Jews to the Bełżec death camp; the site where the Germans gunned down thousands of Jews once the soldiers grew impatient with loading Jews on trains. Both genocidal events occurred on August 27, 1942 on the day the deportation order for Wieliczka's remaining Jews was implemented. (Photo in the public domain.)

He agonized over what their situation might be, but there was nothing he could do about any of these outcomes. He resigned himself to their deaths. But, if there was even a 1% chance any of the four of them had survived, he dedicated himself to do his best to survive in the hope he would be reunited with them after the war.

Do wszystkich Żydów!

1) W Wieliczce rozpoczyna się dzisiaj wysiedlanie Żydów.

2) Wysiedleniu nie podlegają Żydzi z żonami i dziećmi, których paszporty żydowskie, względnie zaświadczenia pracy, zostały skontrolowane i ostemplowane.

3) Szpital żydowski istnieć będzie nadal. Chorzy znajdujący się w szpitalu nie będą przesiedleniem objęci. Przyjmowanie dalszych chorych nie jest dozwolone.

4) Każdy żydowski przesiedleniec może zabrać ze sobą 10 kg bagażu (łącznie z gotówką, przedmiotami wartościowemi i żywnością na 4 — 5 dni.

5) Punktem zbornym transportu jest rynek górny Rada żydowska i Członkowie żydowskiej straży porządkowej dołożą starań, by wszyscy żydowscy mieszkańcy miasta dnia 27. 8. 1942. o godzinie 7 rano byli gotowi do wymarszu. Nie odnosi się to do żydowskich mieszkańców, których paszporty żydowskie, względnie zaświadczenia pracy zostały przez policję bezpieczeństwa skontrolowane i ostemplowane.

6) Każdy Żyd, który przedsięweźmie działanie zmierzające przeciwko zarządzeniom przesiedleńczym będzie rozstrzelany.

7) Każda żydowska osoba, która udzieli pomocy przy działaniach zmierzających do obejścia zarządzeń przesiedleńczych będzie rozstrzelona.

8) Każdy Żyd, który usiłuje jakiekolwiek przedmioty (przedmioty wartościowe, meble, odzież i t. p.) Żydom lub Polakom sprzedać będzie rozstrzelany.

Krakau, dnia 26. 8. 1942

Dowódca SS i Policji
w dystrykcie Krakau.

The deportation orders posted in Wieliczka, Poland, on August 26, 1942 (in Polish). (Meiri, *The Jewish Community of Wieliczka*, 92.)

Translated in English

To all Jews!

1. The deportation of Jews in Wieliczka will begin today.
2. The deportation will not include Jews with wives and children whose Jewish passports or work permits were inspected and stamped.
3. The Jewish hospital will continue to exist. Sick patients in the hospital will not be deported. Admission of new patients is not allowed.
4. Every Jewish deportee can take 10 kg of luggage (including cash, valuables, and food for 4-5 days).
5. The meeting point for transport is the upper main square. The Jewish Council and members of the Jewish Order Guard will ensure that all Jewish citizens will be ready to march at 7:00 A.M. on August 27, 1942. This does not apply to Jewish citizens whose Jewish passports and work permits have been checked and stamped by security officers.
6. Any Jew whose actions interfere with the deportation will be shot.
7. Any Jewish person who assists someone interfering with the deportation will be shot.
8. Any Jew who attempts to sell items (valuables, furniture, clothing, etc.) to Jews or Poles will be shot.

Krakau, August 26, 1942

SS Commander and Police
In the district of Krakau.

The deportation orders posted in Wieliczka, Poland, on August 26, 1942

ESCAPE TO THE BOCHNIA GHETTO

Before the news of the deportation of Wielickza's Jews had sunk in between September and October 1942, the same rumors of planned deportation began to circulate in Miechów (phonetic, "Me-ya-chov"). Soon after that, Miechów's Jews were ordered to report to the nearby train station. It appeared the same script would be replayed. It did not matter whether they were hiding in the ghetto or Gita's home. The deportation order would target all Jews located in and around Miechów.

Nathan and Fela weighed their chances. They had no paperwork that could protect them against a round-up. They considered appearing like orphaned, abandoned children, but without papers they had little to protect themselves if questioned by authorities. So, they again considered running away in advance of a Miechów round-up.

Gita knew it was highly unlikely anyone remained in Wieliczka to care for Nathan and Fela. Gita had heard no Jews were left in Wieliczka, so sending the children back there was not an option. But staying in the Miechów Ghetto was not an option either. Hiding in Gita's home in Miechów was too dangerous in the face of deportation orders since Gita would be required to present herself.

The decision was easy. The two children would have to run once more.

Once again, Nathan found himself saying, "I want to live." The only choice was to be on the move once again. He told Fela this was the only way to survive.

Soon after that, the two children said goodbye to Gita and her family. They made their way to a train station near Miechów. They decided to go to nearby Bochnia (phonetic, "Bo-ch-nee-ya"). They figured they could hide in the Bochnia Ghetto for a short while and then think of another destination. They were not naïve. They knew ghetto liquidation orders would likely come to Bochnia, too, and that Jews there would eventually receive deportation orders there. Nevertheless, they left Miechów with a familiar set of self-imposed rules: do not wear the Star of David armbands, no Star of David on the back of coats, no luggage, and bring only the clothes on their backs. Off they went into another unknown situation.

Bochnia: seventeen miles east of Wieliczka, Poland.

Upon arriving at the Bochnia Ghetto, the two children entered what looked like a scene of absolute carnage. They saw blood on the streets, some of it splattered from what appeared to be shootings or beatings. As they drew closer to the ghetto, they saw larger pools of blood. They also saw scattered luggage, ripped clothing, shoes, menorahs, Shabbos candles, children's toys, and strollers. The wood and wire main gate that enclosed the ghetto was left open. In dozens of other areas, the gates were damaged or completely fallen.

Photo of the Städtische Werkstätten Workshop located in the Bochnia Ghetto, year unknown. (Courtesy http://www.deathcamps.org/occupation/pic/bigbochnia05.jpg.)

It was a haunting scene. There was no one left in the ghetto. It was obvious they had just missed the liquidation of the Bochnia Ghetto. But the silence and relative calm sat in dark contrast to the imagery. Both envisioned the chaos they had just missed. They could almost hear the screams, the pushing and shoving by frightened people. They could imagine the terror in their eyes. They both could almost the feel fear created by shouting Nazis wielding their long rifles and machine guns. In looking around at the debris, they could almost hear the barking German shepherds. All that remained was evidence of mass panic, Nazi physical abuse, and murder. It was the scene of people having been rounded up and herded away quickly and against their will. However, unknown to Nathan and Fela, between August 25 and 27, 1942 the *Aktion* (liquidation) took place in the Bochnia Ghetto. During a second *Aktion* on November 10, 1942, 150 people were shot and around 500 were sent to Bełzec.[12]

It was mid-day, and the two of them had been on their feet since 4:00 A.M. They moved quickly into the ghetto. They found an empty house to stay in. It occurred to them that they might not be the only ones who thought of hiding in Bochnia and that soon others might follow. Sure enough, over the next few days, dozens of other Jews came to hide in the Bochnia Ghetto. Nathan and Fela needed to find whatever food they could before too many more arrived. They quickly went building-to-building until they had a few days' worth of canned goods, loaves of bread, a few dozen potatoes, and apples. They returned to their new home and hid the food they collected so no one would take it from them.

The dark area of the basement they resided in had a few old cupboards and broken furniture strewn around. Whoever was there last had brought a few bales of hay and tossed it on the floor to provide a softer surface on which to sleep. Nathan and Fela gathered up enough hay to make a small mattress-like bed for themselves. They hid the potatoes they found in bundles of hay.

They stayed in the Bochnia Ghetto for a few weeks. They eventually moved to a dark, dingy basement of an apartment building. There they ate by candlelight while staying hidden. There was no electricity and no

---

12. Megargee, *USHMM Encyclopedia of Camps and Ghettos*, vol. 2, 489.

Scene from the Kraków Ghetto after its liquidation in March 1943, similar to what Nathan saw when he entered the Bochnia and Miechów Ghettos, just missing the deportations there. (United States Holocaust Memorial Museum, Photo Archives #39066, courtesy of Instytut Pamieci Narodowej, Yad Vashem Photo Archives.)

running water. Staying in the Bochnia Ghetto was certainly not a long-term solution, and they knew it. They were alive and happy for that but still surrounded by uncertainty and fear.

Most of their conversations were whispered as they could never be too careful. Non-Jews and Jews alike tended to wander into liquidated ghettos trying to find food or valuables, and one never knew who might report someone to the Polish police or Nazis.

In their long days together, Nathan and Fela reflected on what had already happened to their family. They were both grieving their father's murder. They agreed that their mother and three sisters were likely murdered as well, but without contacts in Wieliczka, there was no way of knowing for sure.

They both cried. They wondered aloud whether they were the lucky or unlucky ones, having survived thus far. Yes, they were alive, but without their family. The seeming permanency of their current disposition permeated most discussions during their meals. They were still children, and instead of figuring out their next move, and to which town or village, they dwelled on the past and what they were without.

They were grateful that they still had each other but were aware that could end at any moment. They pledged to one other that if they became separated that each one would do everything possible to survive so that maybe, one day, they might be reunited.

"SHEMA YISRAEL!"

The Jews who took refuge in the Bochnia Ghetto eventually set up a make-shift shul. It was constructed to not look like a shul. The synagogue was in the basement of a house without windows so that candlelight would not be seen from the outside. By the end of October 1942, perhaps one hundred Jews were hiding in the Bochnia Ghetto. Nathan would go to shul at least once a day, say *kaddish* for his family. He did not know if he was saying it for his father alone or for his father, mother, and three sisters. Not knowing weighed on him every day. He was not the only one needing to say *kaddish*, as nearly everyone hiding in the ghetto had already lost loved ones.

One day during the *shacharit* (morning) service, it came time for reciting the *Shema*, the most important prayer in Judaism. The adults there this day sang the prayer with extra loud voices, seemingly unafraid of being heard. They raised their arms to the sky, making a motion that looked like an appeal to G-d for help. Nathan never heard the *Shema* sung like this before with such gripping desperation. Some men then linked their arms together and swayed. Others draped their talisim (Jewish prayer shawl) over a nearby stranger. They formed a huge canopy of talisim, rocked back and forth in looking for G-d. Nathan had not seen such a bond of togetherness, of Jewishness, in three years. There had been no synagogues for Jews to attend since September 1939. For a moment, it was as if the gathering of a small number of Jews stood and sang in resistance as if to say, "we are still here! We pray to G-d even still."

This was the first positive religious emotion Nathan had experienced since the war broke out. It gave him some hope that people were still willing to resist their tormentors in some measure in the face of near-certain death.

After two weeks, word began to spread inside the ghetto that a second Nazi sweep was about to hit Bochnia. Looking for stragglers after a massive liquidation phase was a signature tactic by the SS. But the timing of second sweeps was frequently changed to catch unsuspecting Jews that perhaps grew complacent thinking they had evaded a Nazi sweep.

During their third week in the Bochnia Ghetto, the two children discussed their next destination. During a dinner in their dark basement, they heard a soldier's boots stop just above their street-level basement window. They could not douse their candles quickly enough as it had already attracted the soldier's attention. The soldier knelt, peered into the basement, and saw both children. He then broke the window with the butt end of his rifle. He took three quick shots in various directions and yelled in German, "*Du fauler Juden*!" ("You rotten Jews!")

Miraculously, none of the shots struck either of them, but they immediately ran for their lives. They left behind what food they had accumulated, never intending to come back to the ghetto. They exited the doorway and instead of taking a quick left or right, they ran up a flight of steps to street level. Whichever way they chose to go had to absolutely be the opposite of the way the Nazi would go, assuming he pursued them, which they had to count on. Up the stairs they went. They took a left through a doorway, ascended another flight of steps and quietly pushed open the door to the alley. They were careful to let the door close silently behind them before they bolted away. They did not hear any sounds of pursuit but kept running.

THE END OF HIDING BETWEEN GHETTOS

Nathan and Fela decided to go back to the Miechów Ghetto, which they figured had since been liquidated as well. Once they stepped outside of the Bochnia Ghetto, they had to pretend that they were Christian Poles once again. They would not don the Star armbands, carried no luggage, and proceeded to walk calmly, showing no fear to not look out of place. They went back to the Bochnia train station and purchased tickets, and headed back to Miechów.

Ghettos in the Kraków Region, 1939-1943: Nathan was in the Miechów, Bochnia and Kraków Ghettos between 1942 and early 1943 [see black arrows]. (Courtesy Geoffrey P. Megargee, *The United States Holocaust Memorial Museum Encyclopedia of Camps and Ghettos*, vol. 2, 481).

As predicted, the Miechów Ghetto had also been liquidated. The two children had no way of knowing that on September 4, 1942 "the great *Aktion*" had taken place in the Miechów Ghetto. Between 800 and 900 Jews were sent to labor camps at Prokocim and Płaszów, the rest were put into freight cars "sanitized" with a dusting of lime and transported to the death camp at Bełżec.[13] So there were no Jews left in the ghetto. Instead, they came upon the same surreal and bloody scene in Bochnia, with remnants of turmoil and terror littering the streets. It would be easy for them to sneak in and hide there, but they were running out of options since all ghettos were being liquidated. Again, hiding in a liquidated ghetto was not a safe option because of the Nazi second sweep system. So they had to do something different. But without papers, without any connections or money, what could they do to survive?

As they arrived back in Miechów, they ran into a friend of Joseph Poremba's extended family. This Christian Pole informed them that Nathan and Fela's cousins, the Bakalarzes, were looking for any family who might be alive in either Miechów or Wieliczka. The man told them their cousins were in Kraków and to take the train there. The children were low on zlotys and did not have enough for two train tickets. The man reached into his pocket and handed them money enough to cover the train to Kraków. He told them to head to an apartment a few blocks from the Kraków Ghetto, where they would be able to find the Bakalarzes.

---

13. Ibid., 541.

CHAPTER SEVEN

MY NAME IS STASZEK SURDEL

ASSUMING THE IDENTITY OF A
GENTILE ON FALSE PAPERS

In late 1942, the children arrived in Kraków. They headed to the apartment on the information the family friend provided. The Bakalarzes were the children's cousins on their father's side of the family. There they found Benek, Leo, Max and Itzik Bakalarz.

The four Bakalarz men were classified as "essential workers" for the Nazi war effort. They had jobs in an area outside of the Kraków Ghetto near the airport, working for German officers. They made the officers' custom leather shoes, belts, equipment bags, wrist watch straps and purses for their wives.

Due to their positions, Nathan's cousins were provided papers that permitted them to travel around Poland without being stopped. They traveled to accumulate the necessary raw materials, goods, and tools for leather orders the SS placed. These papers protected them from being deported. They had immunity from being questioned by the Gestapo, even the Polish police.

The cousins had previously found out from Gita that Nathan and Fela were alive and scrambling between the Miechów and Bochnia ghettos and were without papers. They knew Nathan and Fela could no longer shuttle between ghettos safely. The Bakalarz cousins also knew they could not safely shelter the two children.

The cousins encouraged Nathan and Fela to sneak into the Kraków Ghetto and stay there temporarily while they thought of something.

Nathan and Fela agreed because there was nowhere else they could safely find refuge, and they had yet to come up with a long-term plan of their own. Moreover, it was the fall of 1942, and the Kraków's Ghetto had not yet been ordered for liquidation.

Finally, Leo Bakalarz had an idea. Leo knew a priest in Miechów he felt might help. One day Leo went to see the priest. He entered the church and motioned to the priest if they could speak in private. When alone outside of the church, Leo asked for his help in hiding two family members. The priest initially protested that he had no way of helping, but Leo offered him money. The priest said he might be able to help.

Leo offered the priest 500 zlotys, a lot of money in 1942 wartime Poland. The priest then motioned that the two should go back inside. In his office, the priest pulled from his drawer birth certificates of two dead Polish children, one a young male and the other the boy's sister. The priest whispered that the two Polish children had been killed a few weeks ago and that their parents had been killed a few months before that. Both deceased Polish children were close in age to Nathan and Fela. Leo paid the money to the priest who gave him the two dead Polish childrens' birth certificates.

Leo approached Nathan and explained that his best route for survival was to take on the identity of a Christian Pole. He would have to "become" a Christian Pole, maybe forever, if he wanted to live. At the same time, he promised himself he would never surrender his Jewish soul to a piece of paper with a strange name on it. Was this what he bargained for when he told his mother he wanted to live? Was this what he signed up for, pretending to be someone he was not?

The children resigned themselves to doing whatever was required to survive. They owed it to their father, to their mother, and their three sisters.

AN APPRENTICE IN THE SHOE BUSINESS

For the moment, neither Nathan nor Fela dwelled on the awkwardness that came with taking on new identities. But, instead of looking at it as if it were a jail sentence, they chose to look at it as an opportunity. Now they were "legitimate" with paperwork and could move freely.

Nathan took the name "Staszek Surdel," (phonetic, "Sta-shek Surdell"), and Fela took the name "Zosha Surdel," the names on the papers given to them by their cousin Leo.

Both memorized the basic information about their new identities. They had to know the city and date they were born, what their parents' names were, and names of the schools they had attended. They had to be creative and come up with back-stories if ever pressed for details by authorities. They had to have their new life scripts memorized and have the information flow without being nervous. They also had to absorb the fact they were posing as Christians. This meant never reacting to or showing any emotion to the antisemitism they saw and never preparing for a Jewish holiday. They also had to learn the rudiments of Christianity.

They were both battle-ready and schooled in hiding their true feelings.

Nathan's cousins thought it would be best to split the two children up and find each of them work. Again, there was no credible way for the Bakalarz brothers to work for the SS with two new children around. They had to move them.

Fela was placed in a Kraków home as a housekeeper. Nathan was paired with a leather shoemaker, a Pole named Urich (phonetic, "U-riq"), to work as an apprentice. The Bakalarzes sometimes used the shoemaker for certain spare leather parts.

On the day these arrangements were made, Fela left the Kraków Ghetto alone. She said her goodbyes to Nathan, reminded him to keep himself alive so they could be together once again. He would work in Urich's shoe shop, but he would have to live in the ghetto. That posed its own risks. If Nathan were ever followed from the ghetto, they might see where he worked. That could lead to questioning, and eventually discovery that he was a "Christian Pole" named "Staszek." That would beg the question of why a Pole was coming and going from a Jewish ghetto. So, Leo instructed Nathan to carefully sneak in and out of the ghetto not to be identified as a "Jew" coming from a ghetto. Of course, he had to be perfect in his comings and goings, but how?

A few days later, it came time for Nathan to once again leave the ghetto but this time for his first day of work. Instead of sneaking out through a window or an abandoned guard station, the Kraków Ghetto

Krakow Ghetto, main gate, where in 1942 Nathan Poremba snuck in and out under the cover of a large group later known as they "Schindler Jews." (United States Holocaust Memorial Museum Photo Archives #73170, courtesy of Instytut Pamieci Narodowej, copyright of the United States Holocaust Museum.)

Another view of the Krakow Ghetto main gate. (United States Holocaust Memorial Museum Photo Archives #73171, courtesy of Instytut Pamieci Narodowej, copyright of the United States Holocaust Memorial Museum.)

had recently become much better patrolled by the Germans. He learned to time his departure to coincide with the departure of a large work contingent, this group's daily exit. Going out with them provided him the perfect camouflage. He packed himself within the group and walked out without being noticed. When it was time to return to the ghetto, he timed his re-entry to coincide with the group's return. At the time, Nathan had no idea that this large group of Jews was Oskar Schindler's factory workers, a group that numbered over 1,200 people at its peak. The daily crowd made for the perfect cover for a small boy.

On his first day, Nathan walked to Urich's shoe store with his new birth certificate stuffed in his pocket. Nathan's cousins had told Urich that they had the perfect helper for him, willing to work for free because he wanted to learn the shoe trade. Without technical skills, Nathan first swept floors, ran errands, and slowly learned the leather trade as an apprentice. Neither Urich nor his other shop assistant knew Nathan was Jewish. They believed he was "Staszek Surdel" and thought nothing of it.

A few weeks went by without incident. Nathan would sneak out with the "Schindler Jews," and time of his return to coincide with the large group's return. But one morning, the Gestapo knocked on the shop's door. Nathan's heart pounded when Urich opened the door, greeted the officers, and let them in. Nathan assumed the worst. He believed his cover had somehow been blown and that the Gestapo was there to take him away.

However, the Gestapo was not looking for him but Urich's other assistant. Nathan understood some German and could not completely make out why they were looking for the man. But the Gestapo pressured Urich to show them where the assistant was. He acquiesced and took them to the back of the shop where the assistant was. The Gestapo took the man away without explanation and never even looked in Nathan's direction.

This encounter frightened Nathan. As the Gestapo asked questions, he could not fathom being able to deal with them had they questioned him. He had so much to hide. Polish cities crawled with the Gestapo, so Nathan resigned himself to leaving Urich almost as soon as he started working there.

Nathan came up with an idea to remove himself from danger as best he could. He thought he would find work in a nearby village. The Gestapo typically paid fewer visits to rural areas, and he determined that work there was better suited to him. He could not let on that the Gestapo's visit shook him.

Nathan composed himself a few days later as best he could and approached Urich. He told him he wanted to find another job explained that he had no shoe or leather working experience and could not be the assistant Urich needed. Urich appeared to buy his argument.

Nathan knew he could not just walk out the door without a destination or a plan. So, he asked Urich if he knew of anyone that needed a helper or assistant outside of Kraków. Urich said he knew a peasant in a nearby village who had a farm who might need a farmhand. He said he would take Nathan there and see if the man could use the help. Then, to help cement the move, Nathan said, "I can work for free for him, too." Urich had no idea why Nathan was so eager to work for free in another job that would almost certainly require much more physical labor than was required in a shoe shop, but Urich was happy to oblige Nathan.

A Slave on a Farm in Bibice

It was the beginning of 1943 and bitterly cold, as cold as any winter Poland had ever seen. But, as promised, Urich took Nathan to the peasant he knew in Bibice (phonetic, "Beh-bitz-eh"), a village located about five miles northeast of Kraków. Before going, Nathan went back to the Kraków Ghetto one last time, sneaking in with the Schindler Jews. He wanted to leave word with a few people where he was headed. He asked that they get a message to his Bakalarz cousins letting them know he left Urich's shop and went to go work on a farm in Bibice.

He dared not risk sending a message to his sister. She had to remain in character, and he did not want to disrupt that or worry her. So he spent the night in the ghetto and, by morning, exited with the Schindler Jews as they left for work.

Nathan understood that the farm in Bibice might not be his final stop, but Bibice felt like a safer choice to him.

In the back of his mind, Nathan knew it would not be long before the Kraków Ghetto was also liquidated. He wanted to be as far away from the ghetto as possible.

It was a short horse and buggy ride to Bibice. Urich did not want Nathan riding with him because it might look suspicious. Urich wanted no trouble for himself or to be seen traveling with a small child. So Urich instructed Nathan to follow on foot for a few miles, so it did not look like the two were traveling together. Once they were far enough outside of Kraków, he motioned to Nathan and allowed him onto the buggy. All

Bibice: five miles northeast of Kraków, Poland, fourteen miles northwest of Wieliczka.

Nathan possessed were the same clothes he had been wearing for a few years. Draping over his small frame was a tattered and dirty shirt, pants that were a size too large for him, and an overcoat whose lining was torn on the inside. Nathan had already lost about fifteen pounds of weight in the three years since the outbreak of the war.

When Urich and Nathan arrived at the farm in Bibice, Urich said to Nathan, "Just play along with what I say to the farm owner." Nathan agreed as he was confident Urich would help him due to his relationship with the Bakalarzes. The buggy came to a stop, the two disembarked, and approached the farm owner, a man named Joseph. Urich introduced Nathan to Joseph.

Urich said, "This is my nephew; he's looking for work. His family is all dead."

That was Nathan's cue. "Hello. My name is Staszek Surdel," Nathan confidently said, introducing himself.

Urich asked Joseph if he could use a farmhand willing to work for free. Joseph seemed interested. He explained the farm belonged to his brother, who was in the Polish army, had been captured by the Germans in 1939, and was in a prisoner of war camp. He said he was trying to keep his brother's farm afloat and had no money to pay a farmhand. That seemed like a "yes," but he demanded to know more about this boy who miraculously showed up on his doorstep.

Joseph asked Nathan for his papers. This was not an odd request because not carrying papers during the war was suspect. Joseph clarified and said, "I heard stories of Jews being hidden on farms." He made it clear he was not looking for this kind of trouble and did not want to be shot for hiding a Jew. This did not disturb Nathan one bit, who was quick to hand Joseph his papers. As Joseph grabbed Nathan's papers, he quipped, "Jews live in cities. You're not from a city, Staszek, are you?" as he gazed at the birth certificate.

Nathan was ready for these types of questions. He had rehearsed his answers. He could not let slip and accidentally answer too fast and blurt out "Wieliczka," he had to stay in character and in line with his false papers. Nathan said, "No, I'm from a nearby village." "Good!" said Joseph.

Satisfied that Nathan was a Christian Pole, Joseph agreed to the arrangement and took Nathan on as a farmhand. Again he said, "I'm not paying you, remember that, but you will work hard for me, or I will cut you loose." Urich and Joseph shook hands. Urich then patted Nathan on the back and said, "Keep warm and good luck here." That was the last Nathan ever saw of Urich.

Joseph was single, in his early thirties, and a habitual drunk. He saw his role as maintaining his brother's farm until he returned. He was not looking to set any records in farm production and only cared about keeping the farm above water for his brother. He made all this clear to Nathan. He expected Nathan to work hard so that he did not have to. It was a ten-acre farm, a fair size piece of land with two cows, two horses, two bulls, and a dozen chickens.

Nathan did not learn until the next day that the farm was required to provide milk and eggs to nearby German soldiers stationed in Bibice. "Will it be a problem, Staszek, delivering milk and eggs to the soldiers up the road every day?" Nathan was stunned and pretended he had not heard and asked Joseph to repeat what he said. Joseph clarified, "I hate the Germans; they are holding my brother and many other Polish heroes. They came to the farm and ordered me to bring them dairy products. I don't have a choice in this, but better you take them over, so I don't have to see their cursed faces."

Here Nathan thought he was leaving Kraków to get as far away as possible from the Nazis. Now he found himself a stone's throw from German soldiers. On top of that, his new job required him to deliver milk and eggs to the soldiers directly. "No, it is no problem. I can do it," said Nathan. What else was he going to say?

The sheer weight of having to survive was weighing on Nathan. Every time he had run and relocated somewhere, before he knew it, he had to run again. This time he thought he was getting as far away as possible from Germans but instead realized he was now living near a German fortress and defensive line. If that was not enough, he had to visit the soldiers and bring them food. There was no opportunity for him ever to feel secure. The mental and emotional stress was enormous, but he had to play along if he wanted to live. The worst feeling, however, was what surprises lurked around the corner for Nathan. "What dilemma would I face next?" crept into his mind nearly every minute.

Nathan had just left the Kraków Ghetto immediately before the third and final liquidation. He had no idea that his plan to escape the city for the assumed safety of countryside was right before the bloodiest and last liquidation of the ghetto. The liquidation was personally supervised by SS-Sturmbannführer, Willi Haase, and carried out by SS-Sturmführer, Amon Goeth. It began on March 13, 1943. The able-bodied from Ghetto A, at least 8,000 Jews, were marched to the nearby Płaszów labor camp. The remaining people, including all the inhabitants of Ghetto B, were either murdered in the ghetto or transported to their deaths, with over 1,000 Jews being sent to the Auschwitz concentration camp.[1]

Improvisation Skills of a Thirteen-Year-Old

Nathan had no experience in farming. He had only lived in a city and never tended to livestock. He had to adapt and take on the role of an experienced farmhand if he was going to fool Joseph and remain hidden on his farm.

When Joseph asked him if he knew how to milk the cows and harvest crops by hand, he naturally said he could. But in truth, he did not. So, to cover up his lack of know-how, he told Joseph that while his family had a farm, his sisters and mother did most of the work. So at least he had gained some experience helping his sisters. Nathan then asked Joseph to remind him how to milk a cow. He promised Joseph the skills would come back to him very quickly.

Joseph showed Nathan how to milk the cows, collect eggs, plant and harvest corn and potatoes, feed the animals, and have the bulls mate with the cows. Nathan paid careful attention as Joseph did these tasks. Within a few days, he earned Joseph's trust. Nathan, always on guard, felt like he could finally settle in on the farm. If he kept his head down, did not talk much, and just did his job, he could put Joseph at ease so that he could go back to his drinking and sleeping late.

1. Megargee, *USHMM Encyclopedia of Camps and Ghettos*, vol. 2, 530.

Nearby peasants often frequented the farm and dealt directly with Nathan on farm business. They would order a calf or place an order to have their cow mate with one of the bulls. Sometimes neighbors would need extra feed or milk and eggs and pay Nathan for it. Nathan learned the prices of the products and for the other services. A few of the neighbors were nosey, never having seen Nathan before. The peasants pressed him early on and asked him where he was from, his name's origin, where his parents were. He handled the questions easily, having expected them. By comparison, he was considerably less intimidated by the village's nosey neighbors than by a surprise visit from the Gestapo.

Always at the ready, Nathan stuck to the same script: "My mother died of tuberculosis just before the war. She was very sick." In fact, there had been a tuberculosis outbreak in the late 1930s, and he used what he knew about the outbreak to fit his narrative. "What about your father? Did I know him?" peasants would often ask. Nathan had a response at the ready for this, too. "My father was killed in a terrible train accident." Train crashes were a common occurrence in pre-war Poland. No one would question that his father died this way. "Any siblings?" the neighbors would ask. "Yes, but they all died in 1939 during the German invasion. They died in a bombing raid during the opening air blitzes."

No one ever suspected or asked if he was Jewish. The name "Staszek Surdel" was not a Jewish name. By thirteen, Nathan's hair had become a brownish blonde. He still had his blue eyes and was small for his age. But, nothing about him stuck out as being Jewish to them.

Nathan had his own room in the farm's main house, but it was not a finished room. That part of the main house was built from logs with two-inch gaps between most of the logs. His room was an add-on structure Joseph's brother was unable to complete due to the war. As a result, the room did not retain any heat. Poland's harsh cold winters took their toll on Nathan. Blizzards routinely blew snow through the gaps, and most mornings, he would wake up covered in an ice blanket. All he had was a beat-up long winter coat and shirt to sleep in. There were no blankets and no pillows. Those were luxuries that were not available. His bed was made of straw from the barn floor where the animals were kept. Every morning he would re-gather straw that came loose during the night and pack it as tight as possible. He would add more straw from the barn on occasion but not too much to attract Joseph's attention.

Nathan had a bad case of lice he had picked up from living in the Kraków Ghetto and no medicine for this. His clothes had long ago become rags hanging on his skinny, malnourished frame. He had no access to warm water for a bath and since the ground water was ice cold in the winter was unable to bathe himself during the winter months. His body was covered in sores and lesions from lack of bathing and clean clothes. In rural Poland there was no way to obtain medicine or see a doctor. In the countryside, Nathan would have to make do.

The farm sat on a hill above a small valley. A half dozen smaller hills surrounded the valley. When the sun set, the last rays of light shone on Joseph's farm, while below the rest of the village would slowly darken into night. This might otherwise have made a beautiful scene: in a three-hundred-and-sixty-degree circle below the farm sat a series of small round hills. Those hills framed the farm, which became dark green in the spring with lush grass, turning to a golden hue in the fall. Dirt brown roadways lined the valley below, which served as a stark contrast to the thick green grass or the blinding snowbanks in winter.

On the hill that held up Joseph's farm and at its center was the main and only building, made up of old unfinished wood formed into log-cabin walls which were well sealed. Most of Nathan's room was made up of these log walls.

To the south of the building was a narrow road that led down the hill to the central road. An artery to the east was the path two cows and two bulls took in and out of a paddock. Some chickens were kept in a coop near the cows, and others were kept inside the main structure in the center of the farm. A small dense forest sat to the east of the farm down the hill.

Behind the farm's main building was a field where potatoes were planted along with some corn.

Down the hill to the northwest were two above-ground fortresses that were heavily walled. These fortifications were remnants left over from the Great War, but they had been built between 1895 and 1897 by the Austro-Hungarian empire. During the Great War, the Germans added on to the fortifications and built an intricate set of tunnels below. The fortress above ground was split below into three tunnels below ground that all converged on the inside beneath the hill where Joseph's farm sat. The Germans had recently re-fortified their subterranean Bibice-village fortress. German soldiers crawled underneath the farm where Nathan was hiding. This strategic fortress made Bibice a doorstop to potential foes. It was meant to function as a defensive line.

Ironic that Nathan previously escaped the Nazis in Wieliczka, then again in Miechów, evaded them in Bochnia, once more in Kraków only to find himself on top of a hill teaming with German soldiers below. Nathan only learned of this situation after settling into his job as a farmhand.

"Fortress 45a Bibice" was built between 1895 and 1897 as part of the Austro-Hungarian. Festung Krakau. Re-opened by the Nazis, the underground fortress's artillery consisted of 4 *Senkpanzer* M.94 8cm gun turrets and housed 250 men. In 1944 the Nazi fortress in Bibice was defended by the Nazis stationed in Bibice and joined by a German garrison from Kraków who fell back to fight against the Red Army. The Russians surrounded fortress-Bibice and fired with heavy howitzers on it. After a couple of direct hits, the Nazis at the fortress wall surrendered. (Courtesy of Adam Kurelewicz, http://www.fortyck.pl/fort_45a_bibice.htm.)

"Fortress 45a Bibice." (Courtesy of Adam Kurelewicz, http://www.fortyck.pl/fort_45a_bibice.htm.)

Another view of the German fortress Nathan Poremba delivered dairy products to from the nearby farm he hid and worked on in Bibice, Poland. (In the public domain and courtesy of https://commons.wikimedia.org/wiki/File:Fort_pancerny_45a_%22Bibice%22_.jpg; and at https://www.tracesofwar.com/sights/4759/Festung-Krakau---Fort-45a-Bibice.htm.)

As the saying goes, "the closer to danger you are, the farther from harm you are." For the moment, at least, this corollary appeared to be true. The Germans in Bibice were not there to hunt for Jews. They were stationed as a defensive force with their eyes and guns pointed east to the Russians.

On many a night, Nathan would leave his straw-stuffed sack of a bed and lean his face into the unfinished slits in the log-cabin walls of his room. The spaces between the logs were large enough to see the stars set against the black midnight sky. Unfortunately, the winters were too cold to do this and he would stay in the farthest corner of his room, facing away from the gaps during those months. As a result, he often shivered himself to sleep during the winters.

There was no running water inside the barn or in any of the living quarters. The closest well was more than a mile away from the farm. The nearest out-house was a half-a-mile away. No matter the weather, Nathan was expected to make water runs for the farm. So, he learned to manage and time his personal bathroom needs to this chore. He would struggle in his thin clothing and torn shoes in deep snow carrying jugs of water back to the farm in the cold of winter.

It was difficult to feel like this was home, but for Nathan, it became one. He lived in relative safety. Often, he wondered what was going on in the outside world: who might still be alive? Was there a chance his mother was alive and looking for him? Where were his three sisters? How was Fela doing? Who was winning the war? There were no answers because Bibice was completely isolated. Over time he learned to quell his appetite for information and think only about his duties on the farm because that was his key to surviving.

CUT-OFF FROM THE OUTSIDE WORLD

The room Nathan slept in had only a straw bed and a small chest of drawers, and no other furniture. He had one kerosene lamp that ran on oil. He had no personal belongings except his father's pocket watch. Of course, he also had his false papers, the "Staszek Surdel" birth certificate. The watch came to symbolize Nathan's "sword" in that it reminded him not just of his father, but his family back home. The pocket watch gave him forward purpose and allowed him to think of a tomorrow. It was in remembrance of them that pushed him daily to venture on and to live so that maybe one day he could re-unite with his sister, Fela. The Surdel-papers were his "shield" in that the birth certificate provided him protection from being detected as a Jew. The papers gave him the confidence to represent himself as a Christian Pole and remain on the farm in hiding with credentials that vouched for him.

Early in his stay on the farm, Nathan decided to protect these two items. The only place to put them was in the chest of drawers. He made a small bed of straw in the middle drawer, and on top of that, he put his Surdel-birth certificate to the right and his father's pocket watch on the left. On top of his possessions, he put another layer of straw. He then put a spoon and fork on top of the straw to make it appear these were the only items in the drawer. He would open the drawer and gently part the straw, and pick up the pocket watch at night before he would lay down to sleep. It did not work any longer, probably damaged from moisture and rust, but that did not matter to Nathan. Having the watch that belonged to his father, something he had on his person the day he was murdered, kept Nathan close to his home and family. After holding it for a few minutes many a night, he would carefully place it back in the drawer and gently re-assemble the straw over it. The watch conjured up both joy and anger: joy and love as he remembered his father's hand on his head or holding hands as they walked to synagogue; anger and sadness over his father's murder and the betrayal of their Polish teenage neighbors. His father's pocket watch reminded him who and where he was before the Holocaust, home with his family. The false identity papers were a reminder who he had to pretend to be in order to survive.

Nathan had no news about the war. Everyone knew the Germans had invaded Russia and had occupied much of Europe. But no one in Bibice knew whether the Nazis were successfully holding this territory or not. Similarly, Nathan had no way to know what was happening to the Jews. He could not ask anyone if they heard anything about actions against the Jews. These types of questions were ones only a Jew would ask. But it was not easy for Nathan as he pondered these questions deep into the nights. This was the price of hiding on the farm in Bibice under an assumed identity.

Holding back his emotions was both good and bad. The good was that Nathan no longer lived under the pressures of having to relocate

"Sword and Shield" - his father's pocket watch next to his "Staszek Surdel" false papers which Nathan Poremba kept hidden in a drawer on the farm in Bibice until stolen by Polish bandits; illustration by Bosch Fawstin

from ghetto to ghetto, trying to stay one step ahead of the Nazis. He also no longer had to fear the Gestapo showing up. But at the same time, stifling his emotions was not healthy. Instead, he lived in a state of constant worry for those he loved.

He wondered to himself what sort of world he would find on the other side after the war. Would it be a Nazi-led world without Jews or a Soviet-led world without Jews? If the Nazis were victorious, would he have to remain "Staszek Surdel" for the rest of his life? What if he could never go back to being who he truly was? These thoughts frightened him and made him feel imprisoned within himself.

The only way to make it through seemed to be to try and forget who he was, forget that he was a Jew from Wieliczka.

Freedom indeed requires hope. Nathan was aware of his plight. But he had no idea if it was temporary or permanent. Such a state can dim hope. He could not envision an Allied invasion of Europe, liberation from Nazism, and freedom from being hunted. For Jews, none of that seemed possible, especially to a young boy cut-off from the outside world. He could not afford to get ahead of himself and dream of "one day being free" and with his family.

Nathan also had to conceal the fact he was circumcised. If a Gentile discovered this, it meant certain death. Thus, he never undressed and was always on guard when he had to relieve himself. If Joseph ever discovered the truth, he would surely kill Nathan or kick him off the farm.

Joseph did not share much of his food with Nathan, who mostly ate potatoes, raw eggs, and milk. However, on an average day, Nathan's sole sustenance was cow's milk and nothing else. If it were not for the cows, he would surely have died of starvation on the farm. When there was a little flour, Nathan would make himself pancakes on the stove, but that was a rarity. There was no meat available on the farm. Whenever there was food to make a meal for two, Joseph expected Nathan to cook for them. Since there was no electricity or natural gas, Nathan had to kindle fire with his bare hands from the wood he collected.

Joseph treated Nathan as a slave, not as a friend or an employee. The only conversations between them consisted of orders to "do this, do that." From Thursday through Sunday, Joseph often went away on the weekends to get drunk with his Polish friends up north. On those days, Nathan could relax a bit because the slave driver was gone, but he always left Nathan a list of tasks to accomplish before Joseph returned.

One of the worst parts of his job was taking milk every morning to the soldiers stationed nearby at the Bibice fortress. The delivery was required by German order. While Nathan had rehearsed his fake name and back story about how he became orphaned, he anticipated the questions he might be asked by the German soldiers at the fortress. Luckily, the soldiers in Bibice had grown used to Nathan and never questioned him, not even once. He looked like a frail Polish boy in tattered, dirty clothes to them. However, every few weeks, a new infantry member or officer would arrive who did not know Nathan. There was always a measure of anxiety over whether a new person might decide to press Nathan on his background. There was also always a chance soldiers might simply decide to taunt and pick on a Polish kid. But the daily deliveries to the soldiers were a risk Nathan had to take because Joseph demanded he do it. Any hesitation on Nathan's part would surely have raised suspicion.

NIGHT TERRORS

As the years wore on, Nathan slowly forgot the Jewish holidays and Shabbat. Farming work became routine, as did scrounging for a few dozen calories of food each day. The only things Nathan thought about during the daytime were his farming chores, staying warm in the winter, and finding food. Eventually, feeding the animals, harvesting crops, milking cows, and making daily deliveries to the German soldiers all became mundane tasks. In time he forgot about the war. But at night, that was an entirely different story.

At night Nathan was most vulnerable. Night, and especially the dark, were when memories and longing took hold of his mind and heart.

Nighttime meant ruminating thoughts about his parents. He replayed over and over the times he last saw each of them. His mind painted what they were wearing, what they said. It recreated the shape of their lips, their mannerisms, and the tone of their voices. He slowed it down, sped it up, and replayed these images and scenes over and over. He missed them desperately and could not conceive of life going forward without them. He also longed for his three older sisters and wondered whether they somehow had escaped Wieliczka before it was liquidated. Every night the same thoughts ran through his mind: "Where is my mother? Is she alive? Where are Tala, Sala, and Esta? Are they with my mother?" He had no information from Fela and had no idea if she was alive, either.

Memories, questions, and doubts sometimes gave way to desperation, panic, and immeasurable sadness. Nathan went through this every night for three long years. He cried most nights on his cold, hard straw bed but had to stifle the cries lest he alert Joseph.

Eventually, Nathan learned to cry in silence without making a sound and without producing any tears. He found the easiest way to cope was learning to forget about his family and forget who he was. Forget he was from a Jewish town. Forget he was a Jew.

In time, he forgot his real name and who he was. Slowly, Nathan began to lose his identity.

"I HAD FORGOTTEN WHO I WAS"

Just when Nathan thought he had gained mastery of his feelings over missing his family, missing Jewish life, something would inevitably happen to set him back. He would always have to find a way to snap back from this.

Now and again, peasants from neighboring farms and villages would come by the farm and ask Joseph and Nathan to come to church. Nathan could not say no, or even hesitate with an answer. The answer most always was "yes." But Nathan had never been inside a church before. He had no idea what one looked like inside or what was expected of him. One day he was asked and agreed to go. When he arrived at the small church in Bibice, Nathan saw parishioners cross themselves, so he did the same, imitating their every move. He saw them kneel, and so he would kneel. They would bow their heads and pray in Latin. Then he too would bow and move his lips, pretending to pray silently. If they approached the altar, he did the same.

Sala; Tala; Nathan; Fela; Esta, (bottom row, left to right); Gustava; and Joseph Poremba, (top row, left to right), circa 1931, the second pre-war family photo discovered after the Holocaust.

Coming from a kosher home, Nathan had never eaten *treif* (unkosher meat) before the war. But after church, the peasants would sometimes invite him to their homes for a meal. He had to accept. While it was a luxury to have a home-cooked balanced meal, the menu was often accompanied by a pork dish. To decline would have put him in immediate danger as a Jew because every Pole ate pork. So, Nathan would take a plate of whatever unkosher meat the Poles were having after church.

What choice did he have? Yes, the thought of eating pork nauseated him. The smell and taste of unkosher meat were completely foreign to him, but in time, he looked at this as just another exercise to convince those around him he was "Staszek Surdel." So he took polite bites and swallowed. But he especially enjoyed the soups, breads, and seasoned hot potatoes that were prepared much better than what was available to him back on the farm.

The truth is that by late 1943 Nathan Poremba, as he had been, barely existed. The Jewish name "Natak Poremba" sounded odd as he became so used to only answering and reacting to the name "Staszek Surdel." By the end of the year, he told himself this was how life would be forever. He surmised there would be no Jews left after the war, no matter who won. He had forgotten who he was.

Nathan's resilience and resistance centered on accepting things he could not change. He could not affect the Nazi takeover of Europe, the Nuremberg Laws, and the Final Solution. Instead, he focused his energy on what he could change, namely, his adaptability and attitude. He chose to live and to focus on what he had to do each day to live: his farm chores, keeping his head down, and playing the role of Staszek Surdel. These were the things he had control over. Aiding Nathan was his sense of mission. He pledged to make it through the war to reunite with his sister, Fela, eventually. This gave him purpose and enabled him to keep going.

1944: A DRUNKEN POLISH CRIMINAL

The German Front to the east felt far away to the people in Bibice. To them, danger from a German and Soviet fight seemed remote. Nathan's boss, Joseph, had no interest or money to spend on a newspaper for an update about how the war was going, and it would have likely been propaganda anyways. Nathan was always careful never to ask Joseph or any villager that stopped by for any news. Again, exhibiting any interest in the outcome of the war might have raised questions about Nathan.

But one day in June 1944, an unruly group of five or six Polish men began to frequent the farm. Seemingly coming from out of thin air, this group soon became regular visitors to see Joseph. It was obvious Joseph had a friendly history with them. The group would drink with him and share stories, staying up until dawn carrying on. At its peak, the group appeared on scene two and three times a week. Nathan paid them no attention as they seemed to him to be a gang of robbers, thieves, or wartime opportunists. They never before engaged Nathan, so he kept his head down, went about his work, and ignored them.

But one night, while the men were up late drinking, Nathan heard them talking negatively about Polish Jews. They then broadened the discussion to speak harshly about all European Jews. Nathan then heard them take credit for there being "no Jews left in Poland." He heard them talk about an armed uprising by the Jews in the Warsaw Ghetto. After that, they began to talk about a farm they recently raided and looted. They showed Joseph some of the items they stole. Since they were all drunk and loud, it was difficult for Nathan to separate fact from fiction, listening to their tales and news updates.

On a subsequent visit, they again stayed up late and got drunk with Joseph. Nathan could hear them as they recounted their raids on farms and various other businesses, their stories of stealing food and tools from a nearby farm. Nathan paid no attention and fell asleep.

But on this night, hours later, fast asleep on his straw bed, one of the bandits stumbled into Nathan's room. Nathan was sleeping under his winter coat full of holes which was the only blanket he had. He had fashioned it into a blanket by stuffing the sleeves full of straw which he would remove when he awoke in the morning.

Without any reason, the drunken man grabbed the coat and pulled it off Nathan, who jumped off his bed in fear, ready to run out of the room. Instead, the doorway was blocked by the man who then took out his pistol and pointed it at Nathan. After a few moments of tense silence, the man calmly sat in a chair he had dragged into the room with himself. He motioned to Nathan to sit back on his bed.

The man said, "This is a Polish revolver I'm holding. In case you tell the Germans that we steal things, we will kill you." Nathan had no response. The drunk then boasted, "We kill Jews. We kill Germans. We are not afraid of anybody." Nathan's heart was pounding in his chest as the unpredictable man waved and pointed his gun at him as he spoke. Being awakened in the middle of the night, in the pitch dark, made it difficult for Nathan to tell if the man suspected he was Jewish and that this was the reason he entered his room. Aside from the fact, the man was drunk, why was he bothering Nathan? Did he know the "Surdel" family or something? Maybe he knew and figured him for a spy? Thoughts raced through Nathan's mind, but he had to be careful not to react in advance of any accusation. He thought for sure the man was going to kill him. All he could think to do was remain still, as calm as possible, and to say nothing.

The drunk slowly tamped down his aggression, but he was in no hurry to leave Nathan's room. Even though he lowered the gun he had previously trained on Nathan, the man kept the pistol firmly in his hand. Nathan kept glancing at the gun in the moonlight that filtered into the room through the gaps in the log walls. He watched the man's index finger restlessly sliding on and off the trigger. He was aware the man repeatedly kept wrapping and unwrapping his thumb around the gun's handle.

He then told Nathan he was from Wieliczka. Nathan became stiff as a board, his heart pounding even harder. Shivering in fear, Nathan looked closely at him and, by the moon's light, thought to himself, "I think I know this man."

Indeed, Nathan recognized him as someone who used to live half a block away from his home. However, it appeared the man had no idea who Nathan was. Either he was too drunk to recognize Nathan, or maybe he had long since forgotten him. Without saying much more, the man passed out in a chair, the pistol slipped out of his hand, and fell to the floor.

The episode ended safely, but Nathan worried that the man might recognize him as being from Wieliczka by morning. The only thing he could think to do was to get up early and busy himself in a portion of the farm that took him as far away as possible from the drunk man in his room. Being outed by a band of criminals who were armed and hostile to Jews did not make a good combination.

As fate would have it, the man was completely indifferent to the incident when the morning came. It was almost as if he had forgotten their interaction. The man was sober and approached Nathan in the barn as if nothing had happened. He told Nathan the Nazis were looking for him and his entire group. He apologized to Nathan for scaring him the night before and clarified that Nathan should not report him to the Nazis. Nathan, still wary of the man, accepted his apology and went about his work but with one eye over his shoulder.

A few days later, Nathan opened the drawer in which he kept his father's pocket watch and false papers. He did this occasionally but less often as the war dragged on. He liked to hold the weight of the watch in his hand. It helped him remember his father. He would always put it right back in case Joseph should suddenly appear. Nathan could not risk holding it in bed, falling asleep while clutching it, and having either Joseph or one of his bandit friends, see and steal it. However, one night shortly after the encounter with the drunken bandit, Nathan opened the drawer only to find his watch was gone. So, too, was his "Staszek Surdel" birth certificate.

For days he searched, but both were gone. He was certain that one of the Polish gang members must have entered his room while he was out working and took both items. From that day on, the loss of the pocket watch burned a hole in Nathan's heart. He now had nothing tangible left from his family to touch, caress, and reminisce about. Worse, he thought, he was without his shield, the paperwork saying who he was. But soon, reason returned, and Nathan refocused himself. He no longer needed his false papers. Not only would Joseph vouch for him as a Christian Pole, but so would the other villagers in Bibice who had done business and socialized with Nathan. He had proven himself and been accepted by them as a Christian Pole. At this point, the odds were that no one would ever suspect he was someone other than who he said he was.

After nearly three years of slave labor on the farm, Nathan became accustomed to the monotony of farming. Every day was the same, hard physical work on a farm, a means of remaining hidden and surviving. In his rearview mirror was "Nathan Poremba," as the war seemed without end. By the middle of 1944, it certainly appeared to Nathan this was how the rest of his life would go: in hiding posing as someone else.

The raucous bandit's boast to Nathan that "we kill Jews" was revealing. Even segments of the Polish underground played a role in antisemitism and murdering Jews. They had that in common with some civilian Poles, Polish government officials and Polish police. While independent of the Nazis, they, too, were filled with hate for Polish Jews.

THE NAZIS DAILY MILK DELIVERER BECOMES A POTATO PEELER IN BERGEN-BELSEN AND PŁASZÓW

In early July 1944, Nathan made his usual morning delivery of milk and eggs to the German soldiers stationed near the farm. But, after nearly two years of going undetected as a Jew, he would experience something vastly different on this trip. Upon his arrival, Nathan was immediately confronted by a drunk Nazi soldier he had never seen before. The soldier was determined to question and harass Nathan for his amusement. Nathan tried to be professional, do his job, and not pay any attention to the unruly Nazi. He quickly dropped off the farm's daily rations to the Nazis and made his way to collect a few empty milk jugs. But he noticed no superior officer was within sight and therefore no disciplinarian around to rein in the drunk soldier.

Nathan refused to make eye contact with the Nazi or respond to his barbs and taunts. The soldier then followed Nathan around until he caught up to him. He approached and slapped Nathan on the side of his head. This caused Nathan to spill milk from the full jugs he poured into the Nazi's storage drums. But he kept pouring and ignoring the Nazi, but in return, the soldier kept slapping Nathan's head, causing him to spill more and more milk on the ground. One slap to the head became two, which became five, and then nearly ten.

The repeated head slaps brought back a bad memory for Nathan. He remembered when Polish kids slapped the back of his head as they passed his classroom seat in the first grade. They slapped him because he was Jewish. His memory of that time made him even more agitated, but he knew that was what the soldier wanted. He then screamed at Nathan and asked why he had spilled the milk. Nathan knew he could not run away, but he finally snapped in anger after taking so much physical and verbal abuse. He dropped the milk jug straight down on its base, like spiking a football, and kicked it into the ground in the direction of the soldier. The unintended result was Nathan's kick sent wet mud flying towards the soldier. Much of it landed on and caked the soldier's shiny black boots.

The drunken soldier now had what he seemed to have been looking for: an excuse to assault Nathan. The soldier grabbed Nathan by the back of his shirt and hauled him into a nearby barn filled with artillery supplies. Once there, he punched Nathan in the face over and over. He then rammed Nathan's head into a barn post which caused Nathan to fall to the floor, his head and face bloodied. Two other soldiers followed and tried to hold the Nazi soldier back from committing any further violence. The trio of Germans ordered Nathan to stand up. He barely knew what had happened to him and was in shock and slow to react. They ordered him to board a service truck parked outside their post. By that time, Nathan was close to passing out.

Likely suffering from a concussion, hours later, Nathan awoke in the cattle car of a train in the dead of night. It was dark. The cattle car lit up only by moonlight. Confused and dizzy, Nathan had no idea where he was or how he came to wind up on a train. His face and head ached, and he was dehydrated. There was no one else in the car, and he did not hear any human voices from the cars in front and behind him. Barely able to stand up, Nathan came to his feet and peered out the car window, which was about six feet high. He could barely focus his eyes and could only confirm it was night and that the train was moving, but he had no idea in which direction or to what destination. He sat back down on the wooden floorboards. The boards were damp and worn to the touch. He felt grainy sand and dirt as he ran his palms over them. He touched his face, then his chest and neck, and thought to himself, "I guess I'm still in one piece." He was thankful to be alive. But where was he heading? He knew "why," splashing mud on the solider and/or spilling their milk, but he had no idea what the consequence for this would be.

Nathan had heard stories of Jews breaking through the floorboards of cattle cars and escaping the train. But all alone, weak and beaten, Nathan had no strength to pry up a few boards.

Two days later, the train reached Bergen-Belsen, a German concentration camp. The train apparently had several stops along the way but by sleeping as much as he had, Nathan knew not the exact route it took to get here. Nathan was told he was being treated as a "prisoner of war" for having "attacked" a soldier of the Third Reich. Bergen-Belsen began as a camp for Allied prisoners of war. After it was turned over to the SS in 1943, it became a full-scale Nazi concentration camp that housed Allied soldiers and many other prisoners—until the end of 1944 when Jewish prisoners represented most prisoners. Non-Jews were permitted to wear their own clothing in this camp. So, Nathan was not issued a camp uniform; he remained in his own rags.

For the next three weeks, Nathan worked as a potato peeler in the camp. He was placed in former Allied officer quarters because an order was issued that he was not to be mixed with the general population of the camp. Why he did not know. Then he realized he was being held as a "Polish prisoner of war." His camp job also required him to work fifteen hours a day sweeping and cleaning Nazi officer barracks and preparing food for the camp's prisoners. Most of the time, he peeled potatoes which was a highly sought-after job due to its low intensity. In his brief time in Bergen-Belsen, he was never once suspected of being Jewish.

What Nathan did not know was that the sadistic German soldier who beat him in Bibice was the son of an SS officer. When the officer learned of his son's drunken episode, he ordered Nathan be held for two months in Bergen-Belsen. This was because Nathan's role in delivering dairy and eggs to the Germans in Bibice was classified as essential to supporting the war effort. The officer wanted Nathan to resume his role back in Bibice after a brief time of punishment.

But back on the farm, Joseph had not been told how long Nathan would be held. He assumed Nathan would remain a prisoner. So, Joseph filed a complaint seeking the return of his farmhand. He told the Nazis in Bibice that without Staszek Surdel, he could not sow his fields, feed the animals, and make daily milk deliveries to the soldiers. He told them he was disabled and that Staszek did all the work on the farm, that without him, the farm would go under. Joseph also told the Germans he could not afford to replace Staszek because the boy worked for free and that should he have to pay a helper, it would bankrupt and put him out of business. The Nazis acquiesced and informed Joseph they would retrieve Staszek sooner rather than later.

In a few weeks, Joseph was able to convince the Nazis to move Staszek back to Bibice. The Nazi outpost in Bibice subsequently agreed and officially ordered Staszek to be returned to Joseph. Nathan was put on a train to Kraków, where he would make his way back to the farm. Nathan breathed a sigh of relief. All he wanted to do was get back to life on the farm. It was far better to be a slave there with the relative freedom it brought than being in Bergen-Belsen, a grimmer and more dangerous place by far.

But a week later, a clerical error sent Nathan to the labor camp at Płaszów outside of Kraków instead of heading back to the farm.

When he disembarked from the train near Płaszów and arrived at the camp, Nathan knew not to protest or make a fuss. He understood it was a mistake that he had been sent here, or so he thought. The last official word he received at Bergen-Belsen was that he was being sent back to the farm in Bibice. What could have happened?

Upon his arrival at Płaszów, he told the first guard he saw that he was supposed to be sent to work on a farm in Bibice supplying soldiers stationed nearby. The guard laughed but sent Nathan's message up the chain of command, and within a few hours, it appeared the clerical snafu was going to be rectified. But a few hours turned into a few days.

For his first days in Płaszów, Nathan was kept apart from the Jewish inmates. He knew he could not react to the suffering he saw around him. Having previously trained himself in not reacting to the horrors visited upon Jews, Nathan was able to keep his head down and not exhibit any empathy for Jewish prisoners. Nevertheless, the Nazis made use of Nathan by having him peel potatoes until the information he was wrongly sent to Płaszów was confirmed. Three days later, he was released from Płaszów and driven to Bibice.

Upon his return to the farm, Nathan expressed his gratitude to Joseph. Joseph laid no blame on Nathan regarding the incident with the drunk soldier. He understood the soldier was a sadist. He did question him, however, about the two camps.

Once again, Nathan acted tougher than he felt. He could not let on his emotions after having had a first-hand look at his fellow Jews in Płaszów. He could not let slip how deeply it affected him to see Jews suffer from starvation and beatings in Płaszów. His cavalier, unconcerned responses about the conditions in both camps passed muster, and Joseph exhibited no suspicion.

It was at this time that Nathan realized something about himself. There was no set of rules he could follow to ensure his survival. No handbook or manual explained exactly what to do and when in order to live. So, just when life on the farm became mundane and predictable, a simple daily milk delivery turned into a whirlwind of unexpected abuse and a brush with death.

The Nazi occupation required him to constantly adapt, learn new tactics, take on new roles and play it all to perfection to avoid detection. His life always hung in the balance. As the situation changed, the danger did not. Nothing was guaranteed. The uneasiness of day-to-day living, without sufficient or nutritious food, the anxiety over being discovered and caught, always looking over his shoulder, took their constant toll.

Human nature craves consistency, and most people look for a set of rules to follow daily in order to live and thrive. But the conditions and environment of the Shoah were always changing due to the unpredictable nature of war. Although he was still a child, Nathan could sometimes predict and always recognize the sea changes. Adapting to the changes is what enabled him to cling to life.

A FRONT ROW SEAT TO THE NAZIS CRUMBLING EASTERN FRONT

Compared to his brief concentration camp experiences, the rest of 1944 was much more familiar to Nathan. He was back on the farm and, for the moment, still successfully hiding from the Final Solution's orders to liquidate European Jewry.

Word soon spread in 1944 that the Soviets were beginning to win the war. The Germans were falling back and losing ground, but there was no evidence of this in Bibice. Then one day, seemingly overnight, Bibice became a portion of the German front that saw a violent fight between the Red Army and Germans.

By the end of 1944, the rumors intensified that the Nazis would halt their retreat right there in Bibice at their wall and underground fortress. The Red Army was apparently coming closer to the village each day. But still, there was no visual proof of any of this. It was impossible for Nathan to get excited about it. If there was any increased activity in or around the Bibice wall fortress, it was being done under cover of night. None of the villagers saw any build-up or panic by the German soldiers stationed there.

Suddenly, in early 1945, Nathan heard bombs overhead and machine-gun fire to the east. The echoes from gun shots and bomb blasts were real. This was no longer a rumor. The front was now in Bibice. Within hours German soldiers swarmed the farm, coming up from the underground bunker of labyrinths set beneath the farm. In a frenzy, the Germans were emerging from below ground, taking positions in the above-ground fortifications.

It did not take long for the Red Army to learn the Nazis were digging in at Bibice. Russian bombs soon fell on the farm's furthest acreage. It seemed to Nathan the bombs were meant for the above-ground portions of the fortress. Eventually, foot soldiers from both sides appeared around the farm. Trapped between both enemies, Nathan could not risk going outside or running away while bullets were fired from all directions. Because the farm sat on a hill, Nathan had a front-row seat to the fighting as Germans emerged from the bunker and tunnels below like a colony of ants as they rapidly removed camouflaged artillery.

A half dozen Germans ran into the farm's barn and house to take up positions there. The hill the farm sat on made a good vantage point on the surrounding lower ground of the farm. One German soldier yelled at Nathan to leave the farm, almost as if protecting him. Not knowing where to go, Nathan headed to an adjacent farm a quarter-mile away. Bullets whistled over his head; he hunched his body as he ran. Nathan saw grenades and mortars flying and exchanged between both armies. As he ran, he looked back over his shoulder and saw Joseph's farm explode and become engulfed in flame. He scurried to the neighboring farmhouse and told the people there that his farm was under attack. Nathan stayed there for several hours as the fighting continued. The neighbors had a cellar, and the entire family soon took refuge in it, rushing to stock it with whatever food and water they could move.

For the next few days, the frontline remained right where Nathan was. He was in the crosshairs of death once again as the German and Russian armies were mere feet from him.

He could hear wounded soldiers from both sides moaning at night, their bodies strewn across the Bibice fields and hills. The Germans attempted to rescue their own wounded under the cover of night but often paid for it as Soviet soldiers were lying in wait. In contrast, the Soviets left their wounded to die, leaving them as bait for Germans trying to capture wounded Russians.

From the neighbor's cellar, Nathan saw just about every house, farm, and barn in the area had been completely leveled except the one he was in. By the end of the fourth day of fighting, the Germans in Bibice surrendered to the Soviet forces. They were no longer being re-supplied, and the Soviet force was growing in numbers. It was safe to come out because the Soviets soon left Bibice as they moved west. Some of the Red Army headed to Kraków for the big push and assault there. Warsaw had already fallen to the Soviet Red Army on January 17, 1945.

It was now February 1945, and for the first time in nearly six years, Nathan felt inches away from freedom. The fight in Bibice completely leveled Joseph's farm. The Nazis were no more. While looking at its smoldering remains, he knew he no longer had to work there as a slave. He had no idea where Joseph was, but it did not matter anymore. He was free to leave. He was free to go back to Wieliczka and to look for his family. He was free to look for his sister, Fela. He could look for Jews in and around Warsaw. That is if he could find any Jews.

As he passed by the charred remains of Joseph's farm, it donned on Nathan how odd it was that he had nothing that was his to salvage there.

There was no need to walk around the burned-out structure to look for anything that belonged to him. He had experienced that once before when he left his home on #8 Reymonta. In 1942, he took nothing with him from home to fear being seen as a Jew evading deportation. Yes, he had his father's pocket watch but nothing more. But now, in 1945, there was no more watch, no false papers, no clothes, or mementos. There was nothing from the farm he could take with him as a reminder. The farm had served its purpose, just as the name "Staszek Surdel" had. It was time to move on.

CHAPTER EIGHT

LIBERATION AND THE REALITY OF SURVIVING ALONE

JEWISH REGISTRY IN EARLY 1945

For the first time in six long years, the mood lightened ever so slightly for non-Jews in Poland. In and around the Polish villages and farms, people began to smile, if only a little, as the Red Army swept through. Day by day, there were fewer German soldiers in Poland as they continued to retreat to the west. Nathan was careful not to celebrate, nor could he drop character and let slip who he was. He could not afford to rush off to Wieliczka as it was still important to avoid the appearance that he was in a hurry to leave Bibice. After all, he was still a Jew in hiding, and Poland, occupied by Nazis or otherwise, was still virulently antisemitic. It might look odd to folk in Bibice if a farm boy was in a hurry to leave for the city.

As word reached Bibice that the Red Army had liberated Kraków, Nathan felt a measure of security. Nevertheless, he decided to go to Kraków to see if he could find any Jews.

In Kraków, in late February 1945, he found not one Jewish face. He walked up to businesses once owned by Jews and saw no one inside. He walked to Jewish eateries, marketplaces, and textile stores that Jews had owned and saw not one soul. He went to bookstores that still had Hebrew writing painted on the windows, but nobody. He walked up and down the same streets he once remembered to be teeming with Jewish life, but he saw no evidence whatsoever of Jewish life.

This frightened him. It was not good news to see no Jews in what had been known as "Jerusalem-North." Kraków, the second-largest Jewish city in Poland before the war, showed absolutely no signs of Jewish life. What, he wondered, was in store for him back home in Wieliczka?

Dejected, Nathan returned to Bibice for food and shelter at neighboring farms whose owners had come to know and trust him. Then, he decided he would resume his search again in Kraków the very next day. But he met with the same result: he saw not one Jew in Kraków. So, he again retired to Bibice.

He waited a week before undertaking a third search in Kraków. But he knew this time he would not return to Bibice. Before leaving, he approached Joseph's farm one last time. He looked around at the remnants of the room that kept him safe for years on the farm. He gazed at the spot the small chest of drawers had been where he hid his father's pocket watch. He breathed a deep sigh as if to say goodbye and left the farm one last time.

He searched once more for Jews in Kraków. But nothing had changed, still not one Jew to be found. Not one Jewish-owned shop or business had its lights on or doors open. There was no one. He made his way to the train station, still wearing the same clothes and coat he had been wearing for years, full of holes and tears, filthy dirty. The clothes offered little protection against the cold air. Before heading to the station, he sat down on a wet wooden bench. He was mentally and physically exhausted. There he was, seemingly free, the Germans were gone, and he was sitting in Kraków, shivering from the cold. "What do I do now? Where do I go?" he asked himself.

It was late February 1945. Nathan was a malnourished walking skeleton. He had skin lesions and sores all over his body. For most of the war, his stomach had been filled with acid more often than food. As a result, he developed painful stomach ulcers. The emotional stress he had endured also wreaked havoc on his body. No clean or warm clothing, no access to basic medicine or ability to maintain good hygiene, inadequate nutrition, and yet, he was still alive. He felt defeated by the fact he had found no Jews in Kraków. It was impossible to feel any sense of comfort even though the end of the war seemed upon him. Yes, he was free from slave labor and his tormentors, the Nazis seemingly close to defeat, but he felt no happiness.

He was alone, but as he walked towards the train station, he noticed a commotion on the nearby street.

He saw a man wearing a long green winter German infantry coat. A Red Army soldier with a pistol drawn began to slowly approach and yell at the man. After all, the conqueror, the Russian, had his sights fixed on someone wearing a German military coat. The Red Army soldier screamed in Russian, ordering the man to stop walking and put his hands up. A few nearby Poles yelled in Polish at the Soviet soldier, "He is no Nazi. He is a concentration camp survivor wearing a coat to keep warm! Don't shoot him!"

As the man in the long coat raised his arms up, Nathan could see he was clutching a hot cup of soup inside the long trench coat. Finally, after a brief interrogation by the Soviet soldier, he was let go. He announced out loud that the man had come from a liberated concentration camp and was a Hungarian Jew.

Nathan decided to follow the Hungarian. This was the first Jew he had laid eyes on in a long while. Just seeing him revived something in Nathan, a small fire that made him feel like his old self.

Not wanting to attract any attention from the Poles, Nathan followed behind the Hungarian for half a block. Eventually, they came upon a sign that gave directions to a Jewish commissary or registry. Nathan kept his distance and let the Hungarian lead the way. Soon they came upon a small building where a sign said "Registry." But still, the Hungarian camp survivor had no idea Nathan was tailing him.

Nathan watched the Hungarian go inside the registry. The building seemed safe, so Nathan followed cautiously. There were a few people inside putting their names on a list attached to a clipboard. On another table was a registry of books. At first, Nathan was unsure what the purpose of the registers of names were so he hesitated to put his name down, suspicious this could be a trap. But he also knew the Nazis were in retreat and the Russians in pursuit. Finally, a woman approached Nathan and quietly asked what his name was. Nathan was stunned and did not have an answer. He picked up a pencil to write his name down to buy time, but he knew not what name to write.

"What *was* my name? What was my Jewish name?" he muttered to himself.

"What was it?" he silently asked himself again, frustrated he could not remember the name he was given at birth and carried for nine years before the Holocaust.

The war had robbed Nathan of his identity. He had not used his Jewish name during all his years hiding, having buried his Jewishness. Survival meant forgetting who he was so he could flawlessly act a false identity. However, still alive deep within was Nathan's *neshama*, his Jewish soul. That was still intact. But how did he know it was still there? Simple. The magnetism he felt towards the Hungarian Jew was instantaneous. A Jew following a fellow Jew. This action jolted him to life. The connection to one of his own was an old sign of belonging. It was the first time in a long time he had felt a kinship—a link to his people that was submerged for so long. Rekindled was the longing for a Jewish family. This man was Jewish family even though he was a stranger.

With the clipboard in hand, Nathan slowly spelled his name, "Natak Poremba," on the paper. The lady took the paper, read it silently to herself, and then announced his name out loud in the registry: the first time Nathan heard his name stated in public in a very long time. Another man standing near him overheard, turned to Nathan, and blurted out, "I know you . . . I know you from Wieliczka!"

This fellow was somewhat familiar to Nathan. He had also survived by moving from place to place, hiding in villages and ghettos to avoid capture. He, too, did this for six long years. It was surprising the man was able to recognize Nathan. The last time he saw Nathan was before the war, back in Wieliczka, when Nathan was a well-nourished nine-year-old Jewish boy. Now Nathan was skin and bones and fifteen years old.

To be remembered felt like a huge gift. Finally, another Jew was able to *place* him in Wieliczka, in his home. That gave Nathan dignity and meant the world to him.

In a span of just a few moments, Nathan followed a Hungarian Jew because he was drawn to him, and then, another Jew heard Nathan's Jewish name and remembered him from before the war. Two glorious moments, back-to-back. Maybe this was a new day after all. Maybe there was hope.

Nathan scoured the registry books for his mother's and sisters' names. But there was nothing. He then started over and looked for Fela's name, but again nothing. Finally, the man from Wieliczka consoled Nathan and told him not to give up hope, that there would be other lists to check. He told him not to give up because the survivor lists were just now being compiled.

After they had both registered, they decided to stay together. So they left the registry building and walked a bit, sharing their survival stories. They then hitchhiked on a few horses and buggies, and seven miles (14km) later, they arrived in Wieliczka.

She Said, "Why Are You Alive?" but meant "Why Aren't You Dead?"

Upon their arrival back home, the man and Nathan hugged and went their separate ways. Nathan walked towards his childhood family home. On the few minutes' walk from the center of town to his home, he was dismayed to see he did not recognize anyone. Again, not one Jew. It was disheartening, and he realized that what he saw in Kraków, no Jews, was not an exception. There were no Jews in Wieliczka either.

He hurried to Reymonta #8. He was home. He knocked on the door, his heart pounding. "Who might be in there?" he wondered. A few seconds later, a woman opened the door. She was a Christian Pole that was in her 50s. It was clear to Nathan the woman was not happy to be bothered. The woman stared at his face while Nathan looked over her shoulder into the house to see what he could. He realized the furniture in the home belonged to his parents. Everything looked exactly as he had last seen it in August 1942. How very odd: the setting looked like the Porembas lived there, but they were not there.

Suddenly the woman recognized Nathan. "Am I looking at a ghost?!?" she asked. "Why are you alive?" she added with an unambiguous frown and folded arms. She sounded disappointed he was alive.

"Why" was Nathan alive. Meaning, "why didn't the Nazis catch you, too?" Nathan's presence was suddenly very upsetting to the woman.

The questions were posed with the delivery and inflection of someone who had hoped Nathan was dead, along with the rest of his family.

Nathan looked her in the eye and recognized her from before the war. He answered, "Yes, it's me, Natak. I am alive." In a split-second, Nathan realized the obvious: his mother and three sisters probably had not occupied the home in years, and the current residents understood they had taken over someone else's property. The Poremba property.

Instead of asking her if she knew where his mother and sisters were, he asked the woman whether his mother had left anything for him. "No, no, no. Your mother left nothing behind," she said defensively. "We live here now," she proudly said. She kept justifying her occupancy of the home. "Your family left. You left. We are here now!" Maybe she forgot, but more than likely did not care that his family had been forced out and murdered, that they did not "leave" voluntarily. But such a discussion had no place here. It would fall on deaf ears.

It was strange how the scene beyond the woman's shoulder seemed untouched for nearly three years. He saw kitchenware, furniture, and rugs, all in the same spots as he left them. Even his mother's tablecloth was left in place exactly as it had been in 1942.

He could see what had happened: Christian Poles had moved into Jewish homes after their deportations. Synagogues became storehouses. Businesses became garbage collection sites. Jewish homes became Poles' homes. The woman was quick to defend herself and stated she had been paying "rent" to the Polish government for the right to remain in the home. "The home is Poland's!" she said.

Imagine: a nine-year-old boy survives the Shoah, comes back home, and discovers his government took title to the home and now rents it out to whomever they chose. Was a Jew to take the Polish government to court in 1945? Was a Jew to take the purported new tenant to court to evict her? Not possible as no Jew would have a chance in Poland against a

Nathan Poremba, Budapest, Hungary, 1945, after the Holocaust.

Christian Pole residing in a house formerly owned by Jews who no longer had title to the land.

All Nathan could think about was leaving Poland forever.

A GLIMMER OF HOPE

A neighbor a few houses down saw Nathan and came out to talk to him. Nathan explained to her he had nowhere to stay, pointing at his home and the woman standing in the doorway. The kind woman said Nathan could stay with her as he tried to locate family and friends. In referencing the lady living in his family home, the friendly neighbor said, "It's not as if she thinks you're going to evict her. She knows that cannot happen. She is just upset to see a Jew survived."

This kind neighbor told Nathan that approximately four or five other Jews from Wieliczka had returned before him. She said they too came back looking for family and friends and left quickly after not finding any. They did not feel safe in Wieliczka. She told Nathan these other survivors that preceded his return were in their 40s and 50s and that he was the youngest survivor she had seen.

The neighbor provided a measure of closure on some key facts regarding the liquidation of Wieliczka's Jews nearly three years earlier. The woman told Nathan that when the Nazis ordered Wieliczka Jews to the train station in 1942, and that heavily armed Germans and Polish police enforced this deportation. Some had refused to report to the train station and were machine-gunned. Some tried to escape, and they too were executed. She said a few Jews got beyond the roadblocks and ran into the nearby forest, but those were all caught and shot. She said most of the Jews who were boarded onto trains were sent to Bełżec, a death camp. Others were shot in a large group at the train station without ever boarding a train. She explained she was an eyewitness to the deportation and that the Jewish residents of Wieliczka had been completely liquidated on August 27, 1942. Lastly, she said the only survivors from the city were those who had left beforehand, like Nathan.

Nathan's worst worries were confirmed. His mother and three sisters were almost certainly murdered on August 27, 1942. He had no time to grieve now because he needed to leave Poland as soon as possible. However, there would be time to mourn later.

During his ten days in Wieliczka, Nathan checked the survivor registry without success. Nevertheless, Nathan continued to check, hopeful someone might have information about his loved ones. Finally, on the tenth day, he decided he was to leave Poland. He had already experienced more than enough sorrow and disappointment. But he did not know where to go. There seemed to be no reason to remain in Poland because his immediate family was gone. Most of his extended family were also murdered, over two hundred of them on his father's side of the family. He found none of his Jewish friends and no one in town he spoke to had seen any of them. As he walked around Wieliczka, he saw no Jewish faces.

One day standing in front of the house he was staying in, he looked into the setting sun. In the distance, he saw a woman's silhouette. For whatever reason, he kept looking at the figure, fighting the blinding light to try to identify the person. A moment later, she turned just long enough to reveal her face. It was Fela, and she was looking right at her brother. They had not seen each other in almost three years. She was alive and standing in front of Nathan, separated by about fifty feet.

The two ran toward each other and embraced. They cried to each other, "Where have you been?!?" and "Are you okay?" and "Who else is alive?" but all the questions went unanswered as they continued to embrace one another.

It had been years since Nathan had hugged anyone and felt love in return. His soul had been frozen and cut off from the warmth of life since the day he asked his mother to let him run away from Wieliczka. Now he had his own flesh and blood, his sister, in his arms. Their tears of joy soon became tears of sorrow. They instinctively knew their sisters and parents had been murdered.

Nathan explained to Fela that he believed their mother and three sisters had been killed in August 1942. However, it also did not take long for Nathan and Fela to confirm that every single member of the extended Poremba family had also been murdered in the Holocaust.

Fela told Nathan her story. She explained that after Nathan left that she worked as a maid in a Polish home. Her stay was uneventful until she was arrested by the Gestapo and held in prison in Częstochowa. Her crime? Fela was suspected of being a Jew in hiding with false papers. Rumors had passed around Polish neighbors, which developed into an investigation that led to the Gestapo arrest. For many weeks, the Gestapo interrogated her in a nearby prison, trying to coax her into confessing she was Jewish. They tortured her both physically and psychologically. Even though Fela had learned to cross herself and recite a few Christian phrases in Latin, the Gestapo was not convinced.

The Gestapo continued to beat, interrogate and scare her with false tales trying to get her to name other Jews in hiding. They would blindfold her twice a week, tie her hands behind her back, drag her outside and tie her to a post and threaten to shoot her. The Gestapo would tell her that if she confessed to being a Jew, they would let her go, but she never yielded. These sessions always ended with prisoners standing on either side of her

Poremba, Shlomo, ...
Poremba, Shlomo, Sosnowiec, Poland, Mur...
Auschwitz, Poland | Poremba, Srul, 24/7/1900,
24/7/1900, Hagen, Germany. Murdered in Auschw
Poland | Poremba, Ychak, 1890, Kielce, Poland, N
Poremba, Yosef. Murdered in Wieliczka, Poland |
Yosef, 1902, Miechov, Poland, Murdered in Wieliczk
Yosef, 1902, ...awa, Poland, Place of death unknown |
...804, Place of death unknown |
...uania, Murdered i

Joseph Poremba, *Book of Martyrs*, Auschwitz-Birkenau Museum; and, a partial list of more than 200 Porembas murdered in the Shoah. (Photos taken by Noah Poremba June 2015 in Oświęcim, Poland).

...ron, Warsaw, ...uschwitz, Pol
n, Miechow, Poland, Murdered
ba, Feigel, Miechow, Poland, Pla
oremba, Golda, Warsha, Poland.
| Poremba, Gustava, Wielicz
death unknown | Poremba, I
1917, Kielce, Poland, Murdered
land | Poremba, Itzik, Warsa

oremba, Shlomo, Olkusz, Poland, Pl
Poland | Poremba, Shlomo, 1896, Lo
urdered in Auschwitz Birkenau, Po
Poremba, Tala, Wieliczka, Poland,
uschwitz, Poland | Poremba, Yose
sef, Wieliczka, Poland, Place of dea
rember, Abram, Place of death unk

Gustava and Tala Poremba, *Book of Martyrs*, Auschwitz-Birkenau Museum.

1 | Poremba, Natan,
wn | Poremba, Pola,
nknown | Poremba,
own | Poremba, Sala,
nknown | Poremba

1895, Bendzin, Poland, Place of deat
Arie, Warszawa, Poland, Murdered in Au
Ester, Wieliczka, Poland, Place of deat
Poremba, Gedalia, 1914, Warsaw, Polan
| Poremba, Gucha, Sosnowiec, Polan
Treblinka, Poland | Po...

Sala and Esta Poremba, *Book of Martyrs*, Auschwitz-Birkenau Museum.

being shot dead. She endured three months of this mental torture, all the while without breaking down, without confessing to anything. The Gestapo eventually let her go believing her to be Christian after all. They even gave her back her (false) papers. She went back to the Polish home and resumed working. Since the people she worked for believed that Fela was Christian, and merely falsely accused, they nursed her back to health.

Fela Poremba, Brussels, approximately 1947. (Courtesy Joseph Bacall.)

Nathan then told Fela his survival story. They again cried and embraced. Nathan told Fela their family home was occupied by Poles who claimed they were paying rent to the Polish government. Fela was outraged.

THE DICHOTOMY BETWEEN JEWISH AND POLISH POST-WAR CONDUCT

Nathan told Fela the woman who answered the door at their home on Reymonta was upset he was alive. Fela insisted they try to recover their property. So the two of them set out to do something about their family's home. They located a Russian policeman and told him about the people wrongly occupying their home. They explained that it was their home, that they were both in hiding during the war, and returned to find strangers living in their home.

After the war, Russian police were placed in liberated Polish towns as the Red Army continued to battle their way west to pursue German soldiers. The Russian took his rifle and motioned to follow him to Reymonta #8. When they arrived, the policeman knocked on the door, and the same belligerent woman answered. The officer told her to abandon the premises at once because it was not her home. He said that whatever rent she was paying the Polish government was immediately invalidated. She yelled, "Invalidated by whom?" to which the Russian said, "By order of Stalin." He told her the Soviets made the rules now in Poland. The woman responded, "They should be dead! They were supposed to report for deportation in 1942! They are lawbreakers; they cannot have this house anymore!" The Russian responded, "Pack up your clothes and abandon the property now. You have thirty minutes."

Nathan then spoke up and told the policeman that he and Fela only wanted to search their home, room, and attic for personal belongings and family mementos. Nathan told the policeman he would permit the woman's family to remain.

A compromise was struck. Nathan and Fela stayed in their home for two weeks sharing it with the family that had taken up occupancy in it. Nathan's and Fela's only goals were to build up strength and locate their Bakalarz cousins so they could all leave Poland together. But two weeks turned into a couple of months as they continued to hear nothing about their cousins.

One day as Nathan was walking around town, four Polish schoolboys recognized him from his old public school. Two of them pointed at him and yelled, "*Zhyd! Zhyd!*", ("Jew-boy! Jew-boy!"). The group approached and began to harass him. This time, Nathan responded. He pushed one to the ground and ran. A few blocks later, he saw none of them had pursued him.

A few days later, the same group of four boys again saw Nathan out in public. They approached him again, looking for a fight. One said, "Let's have a fair fight, one on one, and see how you do as we each get a turn at you." Outnumbered and unwilling to abide by the boys' rules, Nathan put his right hand in his coat pocket and made it look like he had a gun. He said, "If you come near me, I will kill all of you right here."

The Polish group was fooled and retreated. But minutes later, they began searching for Nathan and found him with two Polish militiamen.

The militia requested the gun from Nathan. "I have no gun, search me," he said. He continued, "These kids are harassing me and making up lies." Finally, the militia believed Nathan and did not search him but warned all the boys to stay away from each other.

A few days later, Nathan faced round three. Two of the four boys were out for a walk and once again spotted Nathan. They approached, taunted him, and again sought to fight. Nathan obliged. With one blow, he landed a punch to one of the boy's face. That boy fell to the ground, banging the back of his head on the street. He lay unconscious, which prompted the other boy to flee in fear, apparently unwilling to fight Nathan by himself. This is what Polish Jews faced after the Holocaust.

Imagine, Nathan survives the Holocaust against all odds. He loses both parents and three sisters. Two hundred family members were murdered on his father's side. The Nazis killed six million Jews throughout Europe, most of them murdered in Poland, while some Poles applauded and cheered, others doing nothing. Some Poles took a more active role, openly volunteered, and assisted in German operations, round-ups, and deportations. Finally, the war ends, and Nathan is back in his hometown. One Pole recognizes him while squatting in his childhood home and boldly expresses disappointment that he survived the Nazi storm. She insists the home now belongs to her. Then, old schoolmates recognize Nathan and immediately, as if on instinct, slur, harass and chase him. Post-war Poland seemed to be no different than pre-war Poland had been for Jews.

It is well documented that after the war there were Polish-led pogroms, beatings, and murders of Jews across Poland.[1] Nathan was lucky in that he did not experience even more hostility. He endured far less but not without experiencing a Polish takeover of Jewish property. Post-war property theft was encountered by most Polish Jews who survived and managed to return to their homes and businesses.[2]

It then occurred to Nathan he still had unfinished business in Wieliczka.

---

1. Jan T. Gross, *Fear: Anti-Semitism in Poland After Auschwitz* (New York: Random House, 2006), 34–38; 81–117.
2. Ibid., 39–51.

Where was the Polish teenager who gave his father up six years ago outside their home? Where was the Polish boy who insisted the German soldier return, re-enter their home, and search for his father a second time? But before he could exact revenge, he had to remember the boy's name to possibly locate him.

Days went by, and Nathan tried but could not recall the name. Nor did he see the boy, now grown up, walking around Wieliczka, either. Even though Nathan knew where the boy had lived, that family was no longer there, nor was the boy. No one had any information on the boy's whereabouts.

Disappointed, Nathan eventually realized that his father would have wanted him and Fela to leave Poland without incident. Joseph Poremba would not have wanted Nathan to commit a crime for him and languish in jail. Fela consoled Nathan that the best revenge was leaving and building a Jewish life someplace else. She explained that leaving on his own terms with a clean slate was the best option. He agreed and let it lie.

CHAPTER NINE

LEAVING POLAND

FLEEING EUROPE ON JARS OF JEWELS

When people discuss the Jewish exodus from Europe after the war, it often reads like a smooth transition. The stories typically flow as if there was persecution, survival, and an effortless arrival at Ellis Island or elsewhere. But few experienced such an easy transition.

With the eastern part of Europe falling under the domination of the Soviets, the western nations were not ready to hand out visas to massive numbers of refugees, particularly to Jews. As a result, it turned out to take tremendous effort for Nathan, and most other Jews, to get out of Europe and make their way to the United States or Israel (the area known then as "Palestine").

Shortly after they decided to leave Wieliczka, in the middle of 1945, Nathan and Fela located their Bakalarz cousins. At the same time, travel within Europe slowly began to open. Unfortunately, the group had little by way of money or valuables. They would have to find a way to scrounge up funds to sustain their existence and train fare. But where would they locate a source of money? It then occurred to Nathan that there was a way to re-acquire some of their long-lost funds.

Before Nathan separated from his cousins in Warsaw and went to the farm in Bibice, Leo Bakalarz had snuck into the Miechów Ghetto. He buried two large jars of cash and jewelry deep in the basement of a ghetto apartment building. The jars contained hundreds of zloty bills of various denominations, gold watches, diamonds, and other jewelry. The items belonged to him, his immediate family, his brothers, and other relatives and were hidden for safekeeping. Nathan was told the location of the jars in case his older cousin did not survive the war. There had been no chance earlier to recover the jars. As far as they knew, the jars were still safe and hidden. Now that the war was over and they were hoping to leave Poland, they needed access to the accumulated wealth. Leo was dead, shot by the Nazis in 1943, trying to escape to the Polish-Czechoslovakian border.

Max Bakalarz approached Nathan and recruited him as the smallest in the group and, therefore, the one most likely to avoid detection in the ghetto. He had significant experience sneaking in and out of ghettos and knew how to avoid without attracting attention, as well as where the jars were located. He was the only one who did.

One cold night at two in the morning, two of the cousins and Nathan set out to retrieve the jars. To the untrained eye, as they approached the ghetto, the scene seemed a low risk. There were no armed Germans out front and no ominous gate with German shepherds. But post-war travel was still extremely dangerous. People were engaged in looting and searching abandoned businesses and homes for valuables and food. The Soviets patrolled the area, and so did the Polish police. Even though the contents of the two jars belonged to them, if the authorities stopped them, their wealth would almost certainly be confiscated. So they had to be incredibly careful. Their chance to leave Europe depended on it.

As they approached the former ghetto, they noticed there were many Soviet vehicles parked nearby. Nathan remembered a backway into the ghetto closer to the apartment building where the jars were hidden. A quarter of a mile later, the three men took to crawling in the bushes and mud. Nathan whispered they were at the back of the correct building and motioned that they should quietly stand up to a crouching position to enter the alley next to the apartment building.

The building was in absolute shambles. It was bullet-ridden with grenade divots on the exterior walls every few yards. The building seemed to be angled to one side as if it were leaning. They entered the rear entrance from the alley where there were no streetlights. No one lived in the ghetto apartments any longer, and no one could be there. They were essentially breaking into the building and violating the law by being there. One cousin remained in the lobby area as a lookout. If anyone approached, he would whistle two blasts so Nathan and his cousin could hide in the basement while the lookout would hide as best he could. Nathan and his cousin went down two flights of stairs to get to the basement where the jars were buried. They turned on a flashlight once they were in the basement behind closed doors where no light could be seen.

The staircase was unsafe, missing steps and railings. There was nothing to hold onto on the way down. The sound of dripping water and the sound of their footsteps added to the tension. Behind a door at the end of two flights of stairs was where Nathan remembered the jars were buried. Once inside, there was old rotting furniture, mold, and dirt. The jars were not where Nathan expected them to be. He pointed at another area, thinking that it was perhaps the spot. Part of the concrete foundation was movable, and under it was dirt. Nathan could not tell if the concrete false door had been shattered from a bombing raid or if the slab was broken apart because someone had discovered the jars and dug through to them. Nevertheless, they fashioned a couple of makeshift shovels and dug a hole nine inches wide until they got six inches deep. The jars were not there.

It was difficult to remember the exact spot. Maybe, Nathan thought, they were in the wrong building altogether. The pressure was mounting the longer they stayed there. They feared they would be discovered as dawn was approaching.

Finally, Nathan fixed his eyes on an adjacent spot. He and his cousin quietly moved smashed wood furniture away from the area. The false concrete door that covered this spot looked somewhat familiar, even if the concrete was discolored by what appeared to be tar. Within a few minutes, they removed enough of the furniture so that Nathan could climb onto a desk and slide down a few feet into what appeared to be a space with broken wood. Only Nathan was small enough to access where the jars might be hidden. He took off his shoes to cushion his steps. The false concrete door was removed easily and revealed a mound of dirt beneath. There was only enough room for Nathan to sit in the cylindrical chute of wood. His cousin handed him the makeshift shovel to begin to dig.

It was now nearly five in the morning, and not much time remained before sunrise. They had to leave the ghetto before daybreak when they could be suspected of being looters. Nathan dug and dug, and six or seven inches deep, the shovel tapped on what sounded like the top of a jar. As Nathan cleared away the dirt, he let out a sigh: he found the first jar. About twenty minutes later, he had dug through the tightly packed dirt and raised the jar. But where was the second jar? He remembered there were two jars, and they were buried next to each other. Alas, the second jar was there, but it was cracked, and the shards of glass mixed with the valuables. It was clear the bombs had broken this.

After handing the first jar to his cousin, Nathan began scooping up the cash and jewelry from the second jar into his lap. Bit by bit Nathan painstakingly removed every piece of jewelry. Every item mattered as it might buy one more train ticket or meal. As he hurried, Nathan cut the fingers and palms of both his hands. Eventually, he removed everything from the second jar. Next, they filled a potato sack with the valuables. Finally, they put the other jar into the sack and used the pillowcase to hold the loose valuables.

Nathan squirmed his way back up the funnel of wood furniture, stood on the wood table, and put his shoes on. The loose items made a lot of noise as they carried them up the building. Nathan tore the pillow open, took out the goose feathers, and packed the jewelry with the feathers. The two made their way back up the staircase, exited the basement, and met their other cousin.

They once again crawled out of the apartment building, into the bushes, and through the mud. When they were far enough away from the ghetto, they looked around. Seeing no evidence they were being followed, they slowly stood up and walked away.

The group traveled from Poland to Bergen-Belsen in Germany because they had heard this was a location where they could obtain the papers for travel abroad. Unfortunately, none of them had their Polish birth certificates. Their papers had been lost or destroyed. They had no proof they were who they said they were, so they had no luck in Bergen-Belsen. A few days later, the group moved to Czechoslovakia, where they tried again to secure the necessary paperwork, but to no avail. They then went to Hungary to try again there.

They remained in Hungary for a year and a half until the end of 1946. Finally, they found work and lived together in a couple of apartments. By 1947, the group traveled back to Czechoslovakia because Hungary was in political upheaval. Once in Czechoslovakia, they saw the same communist turmoil was taking root there as well. Ironically, they determined Poland was a safer place. So, they went to the Polish consulate in Czechoslovakia and obtained the appropriate papers. They were able to all obtain the papers to re-enter Poland, but they could not leave Czechoslovakia because the Russians locked the Czech borders due to a revolt against the communist regime. So, they would have to remain for another six months in Czechoslovakia.

Eventually, the group, now twenty-four strong, was finally permitted to travel back to Poland. Nathan wanted to go back to his home at #8 Reymonta and check the attic again. He remembered there might be a letter stored where his uncle, Alex Ringer, had mailed his mother, Gustava, before the war. He also thought there might be some family photos up in the attic. Finally, Nathan hoped to go to his uncle in New York, as far away from Poland he could get.

When he returned, new people were living in his former home. He explained that he used to live there and asked if he could check the attic. They were friendlier than the last occupants and permitted him to come inside. Nathan found two family photos taken before the war, both pictures shot in 1932. He also found his uncle's New York address on a letter. He could now write to him in New York and let him know he was alive and wanted to come to America.

Nathan and Fela wrote the letter to their uncle Alex in New York. They requested he sign an affidavit stating he would sponsor them to come to the United States. Since Poland was coming under an increasingly authoritarian regime, an iron curtain, they knew they must leave as soon as possible.

As they waited, they decided to go west to Belgium. However, without Polish passports, they would not be able to use Belgium as a springboard to America. Because they were Holocaust survivors, Polish officials were somewhat more lenient and permitted them to leave for Belgium.

From 1947 through 1951, they lived and worked in Belgium, unable to emigrate further west. They felt relatively safe in Belgium. Although, Europe was still unstable and still antisemitic. The group eventually obtained permits to remain in Belgium but still had no way to obtain Polish passports, which were required to leave the continent.

In the meantime, Nathan attended a vocational school to learn various trades. He became certified to do plumbing, carpentry, and some electrical work. Others in the group found textile work and office jobs. Since they were unable to speak French, Belgium slowly became a difficult place for them as Poles. As Eastern European refugees, they did not have it easy in Western Europe after the war due to discrimination aimed at outsiders, something Poland had exacted on its pre-war immigrant class as well.

One of the Bakalarz group, Józef ("Yossek"), relocated to the area called "Palestine." Yossek had survived the end of the war as a prisoner in Auschwitz-Birkenau, where he worked as a member of the *Sonderkommando* (forced to take gas chamber victims to the crematoria for disposal by flame). Yossek and Nathan were remarkably close first cousins.

Feeling out of place in Belgium in 1947, Nathan made his way to Yossek. His cousin had invited him to stay with him. So, for the next six months, Nathan remained in the northern Tel Aviv area. When talk of Israeli independence came in early 1948, along with fear of a massive Arab attack, Yossek, a father figure to Nathan, could not bear the thought of Joseph Poremba's only son losing his life in a subsequent war.

TO ISRAEL, THEN TO THE UNITED STATES

Yossek decided his fifteen-year-old cousin should leave. Yossek told Nathan, "I owe it to your parents to protect you. Enough Porembas have died. You should leave Israel before it gets bad here and you are recruited to fight." However, Nathan did not want to leave his cousin Yossek, a warm, loving, and generous soul. The two debated what Nathan should do. Then Nathan received a letter from Fela, who begged Nathan to come to Belgium right away. She explained there had been an international development that would enable them to leave Belgium for America. When Nathan told Yossek this, their debate ended.

The United States Congress had just passed the "displaced persons" ("DPs") law. This meant the group in Belgium could register as DPs, obtain a special international passport, and emigrate to the United States very soon. The DP Act meant they no longer had to obtain a Polish passport, or even one from Belgium, to be able to emigrate to America. But, as Fela wrote, Nathan had to hurry and return immediately to Belgium to begin the process of completing the DP application.

Nathan went to the Belgian consulate in Jerusalem to try to get back to Belgium. He and Fela had been through too much to separate at this juncture, so if she intended to go to the United States, then Nathan felt he must as well.

It took three years for the DP law to be fully implemented, allowing survivors to be processed for entry to destinations outside of Europe. Since Fela and the group were ahead of Nathan in the application process, they left for America in late 1950. In 1951 it was Nathan's turn to leave for America finally.

Nathan eventually obtained his visa and passport to enter the United

Nathan Poremba, Brussels, Belgium 1946.

Nathan Poremba, Brussels, Belguim 1948.

Nathan Poremba, Brussels, Belgium 1949.

Accord du 15 octobre 1946.
Akkoord van 15 October 1946.

Lieu et date de naissance :
Plaats en datum van geboorte :

Profession :
Beroep :

Résidence actuelle :
Huidige verblijfplaats :

* Nom (avant le mariage) et prénom(s) de l'épouse :
* Naam (vóór het huwelijk) en voornaam of voornamen van de echtgenoote :

* Nom et prénom(s) du mari :
* Naam en voornaam of voornamen van den echtgenoot :

Enfants accompagnant le titulaire.
Kinderen die den houder vergezellen.

Nom — Naam	Prénom(s) Voornaam of Voornamen	Lieu et date de naissance Plaats en datum van geboorte	Sexe Kunne

* Biffer la mention inutile.
* Het overbodige doorhalen.

Ce titre contient 32 pages, non compris la couverture.
Dit reisbewijs bevat 32 bladzijden, de omslag niet inbegrepen.

2

Accord du 15 octobre 1946.
Akkoord van 15 October 1946.

SIGNALEMENT.
PERSOONSBESCHRIJVING

Taille :
Gestalte :

Cheveux :
Haar :

Couleur des yeux :
Kleur der oogen :

Nez :
Neus :

Forme du visage :
Gelaatsvorm :

Teint :
Gelaatskleur :

Signes particuliers :
Bijzondere kenteekens :

Signature du titulaire :
Handteekening van den houder :

Empreintes digitales du titulaire (facultatif) :
Vingerafdrukken van den houder (facultatief) :

Ce titre contient 32 pages, non compris la couverture.
Dit reisbewijs bevat 32 bladzijden, de omslag niet inbegrepen.

3

Nathan's Belgian passport was issued in 1951 for entry into the United States as a "Displaced Person."

Accord du 15 octobre 1946.
Akkoord van 15 October 1946.

PROROGATION DE VALIDITÉ.
VERLENGING VAN DEN GELDIGHEIDSDUUR.

Taxe perçue :   Prorogé du
Geïnd recht :   Verlengd van
                   au
                   tot
Fait à   le
Gedaan te   den
                   Pour le Ministre des Affaires étrangères
                   et du Commerce extérieur :
                   Voor den Minister van Buitenlandsche Zaken
                   en Buitenlandschen Handel :
       Sceau
       Stempel
                   Le
                   De

PROROGATION DE VALIDITÉ.
VERLENGING VAN DEN GELDIGHEIDSDUUR.

Taxe perçue :   Prorogé du
Geïnd recht :   Verlengd van
                   au
                   tot
Fait à   le
Gedaan te   den
                   Pour le Ministre des Affaires étrangères
                   et du Commerce extérieur :
                   Voor den Minister van Buitenlandsche Zaken
                   en Buitenlandschen Handel :
       Sceau
       Stempel
                   Le
                   De

* Qualité, grade du fonctionnaire.
* Hoedanigheid, graad van den ambtenaar.

Ce titre contient 32 pages, non compris la couverture.
Dit reisbewijs bevat 32 bladzijden, de omslag niet inbegrepen.

6

Accord du 15 octobre 1946.
Akkoord van 15 October 1946.

VISAS. — VISA'S.

Reproduire dans chaque visa le nom du titulaire.
In elk visum dient de naam van den houder vermeld te worden.

Immigration visa
Quota Polish   No.
Dated March 13, 1951
Issued to

American Consul at
ANTWERP, BELGIUM

Consular Fee No.

U.S. DEPT. OF JUSTICE
ADMITTED
MAY 15 1951
NEW YORK
N.Y.

Ce titre contient 32 pages, non compris la couverture.
Dit reisbewijs bevat 32 bladzijden, de omslag niet inbegrepen.

7

States. Then, in May 1951, he traveled to America on the SS *Washington*, which had formerly transported American soldiers to Europe. The boat left from France and docked in New York after a three-day voyage across the Atlantic Ocean. As the youngest passenger on the ship, he was the last passenger to disembark.

It made sense that the youngest surviving Jew of Wieliczka would be the last to step off the ship that took him away so far away from the tragedies he had experienced in Poland.

In 1960, Nathan received a benefit award from the German government as a survivor of the Holocaust. He had previously applied for

Aboard the SS *Washington*: Nathan's voyage from France to New York, May 1951.

Nathan's voyage to freedom on the SS *Washington*: International Refugee Organization, May 1951. (Public domain document from the Arolsen Archives, International Center on Nazi Persecution, Arolsen, Germany, archive created with the help of Israel's Yad Vashem.)

Finally Free: Nathan passing the Statue of Liberty while aboard the SS *Washington*, May 1951.

compensation from the German government for being physically and psychologically abused as a child, left without his parents, and forced to do manual labor during the war. The award embarrassingly recognized that his father had been "either intentionally or unintentionally murdered" during the time the Nazis occupied Poland; and that his mother "died on 8/31/42". In July 1960, a letter from the West German government awarded him reparations for October 1, 1939, through December 31, 1948.

However, the West German government only paid reparations to Nathan for his father's murder, not for his mother's. Moreover, according to the post-war law, the government could only pay an orphaned surviving young adult (who was a child during the Holocaust) compensation for losing one parent, but not for both.

Post-War Germany hedged on its language in recognizing Joseph Poremba's murder. There was no full acknowledgment of his intentional murder, no outright unambiguous admission. This was despite the fact the September 12, 1939 military operation rounding up thirty-two Jewish men in Wieliczka was an official act. (An act perpetrated with advanced cooperation and coordination with a Pole that worked for the city). West Germany only partially acknowledged responsibility for its actions in causing his father's death.

However, the letter took no responsibility for Gustava's murder. Recall, Wieliczka was liquidated by official Nazi order posted on August 26, 1942 in the city and enforced by German soldiers along with Polish police. The West German government simply refused to confirm Gustava's murder took place and/or under these circumstances. Instead, the government chose to hide behind a law that Nathan could only be compensated for losing one parent, not two. But by doing this, West Germany failed to acknowledge the August 27, 1942 Nazi liquidation and murder of Gustava on the 27th.

The letter erroneously fixed Gustava's death as being "August 31, 1942." It is unknown upon what information, if any, this was based because Wieliczka was liquidated on August 27, 1942 and at least one witness account, as told to Nathan in 1945, was that Gustava was either shot at the train station that day or sent to the death camp, Bełżec. If the August 31st date were true, Gustava would not have been gassed *four* days later. Bełżec was located approximately 176 miles from Wieliczka, and by train, her murder at the hands of the Nazis would not have occurred that many days later.

Der Regierungspräsident ....   Hannover, den 16. Juli 1960
 - EB - V/R 2 - 1 19598   Archivstr. 2 - Postfach
          - 1 19662

In dem Entschädigungsverfahren

des Natan P o r e m b a
geboren am 25.1.1930 in Wieliczka/Polen
wohnhaft: 561 West 163 Street, Apartment 3 G, New York 32,
                                  N.Y./USA

Bevollmächtigte: Rechtsanwalt Eugene M. E l l e ,
               154 Nassau Street, New York 38, N.Y./USA

ergeht

auf Grund des Bundesentschädigungsgesetzes (BEG)
vom 29.6.1956 (BGBl. I S. 562) folgender

B e s c h e i d :

1) Der Vater des Antragstellers, der 1896 in Miechow bei
   Krakau geborene, am 12.9.1939 in Taszyc verstorbene,
   zuletzt in Wieliczka wohnhaft gewesene Josef Poremba
   (Poreba) ist aus den in § 1 Abs. 1 BEG genannten Gründen
   verfolgt worden und vorsätzlich oder leichtfertig getötet
   worden (§ 15 Abs. 1 BEG).

   Der Antrag auf Entschädigung nach der am 31.8.1942 ver-
   storbenen Mutter Gustava Poreba geb. Lewkowicz, geboren
   1899, wird abgelehnt.

2) Der Antragsteller erhält gemäß §§ 24, 25 BEG eine Kapitalentschädigung in Höhe von

                 2.466,66 DM

   (in Worten: Zweitausendvierhundertsechsundsechzig
              66/100 Deutsche Mark)

   für die Zeit vom 1.10.1939 bis zum 31.12.1948.

Überweisung der Kapitalentschädigung   G r ü n d e :
erfolgt auf das Spezialkonto "Elle und
Salomon" (special checking account) bei
der Chemical Bank New York Trust Company,
165 Broadway, New York.

Letter from the West German Government to Nathan Poremba, July 16, 1960 (page one) awarding a benefit for the murder of Joseph Poremba.

- 2 -

G r ü n d e :

Gemäß §§ 17 BEG, 7 der 1. DV-BEG steht dem Antragsteller bis zur Voll-
endung des 16. Lebensjahres bzw. beendeter Berufsausbildung die Wai-
senrente zu. Zur Berechnung der Kapitalentschädigung war der Vater des
Antragstellers in die vergleichbare Beamtengruppe des einfachen Dien-
stes ausreichend und angemessen einzustufen. Das Unfallruhegehalt wür-
de für die Zeit bis zum 30.9.1951   2.067,-- DM betragen, das Waisen-
geld 620,-- DM oder monatlich 51,67 DM. Da die Mindestrente sich auf
100,-- RM/DM beläuft, ist diese der Berechnung zugrunde zu legen. Für
die Zeit vom 1.10.1939 bis zum 31.12.1948, dem Zeitpunkt der Beendi-
gung der Berufsausbildung, ergibt sich folgende Berechnung:

Vom 1.10.1939 bis 28.2.1946
77 Monate x 100,-- RM =   7.700,-- RM =   1.540,-- DM
vom 1.4.1947 bis 20.6.1948
14 2/3 Monate x 100,-- RM =1.466,67 RM =   293,33 DM
vom 21.6.1948 bis 31.12.1948
6 1/3 Monate x 100,-- DM =   633,33 DM
                                           2.466,66 DM.

Der Betrag von 2.466,66 DM war dem Antragsteller daher als Entschädigung zuzusprechen.

Zugleich war der Antrag auf Entschädigung wegen Schadens an Leben nach
der Mutter abzulehnen, da nur Entschädigung für einen Elternteil ge-
zahlt wird und der Entschädigungszeitraum für die später verstorbene
Mutter kürzer, die Entschädigungssumme daher auch geringer gewesen
wäre.

Hinsichtlich des gegen diesen Bescheid zulässigen Rechtsmittels wird
auf die beigefügte Belehrung verwiesen.

                    Im Auftrage:

                    gez. Schimke i.V.

                                                        /Bok

Letter from the West German Government to Nathan Poremba, July 16, 1960 (page two).

Translated in English, page one.

The Prime Minister   Hanover, 7-16-1960
EB -V/R- 1 19598   Archive street #2 - Mailbox

Regarding the Case for Financial Compensation
For Natan Poremba
Born 1/25/1930 in Wieliczka/ Poland
Residency: 561 West 163 Street,
Apartment 3 G, New York 32,
N.Y./USA

Legal Representative: Lawyer Eugene M Elle
154 Nassau Street, New York

In the case for:

The Federal Compensation Law (BEG)
From 6/29/1956 is the following notice:

1. The father of the application settler, who was born in 1896 in
    Miechow near Krakow (and who) in 9/12/1939, died in Taszyc.
    He last lived in Wieliczka. Josef Poremba (Poreba) was per article
    1 Abs. 1 BEG harassed and either intentionally or unintentionally
    murdered.

    The request for compensation for the mother Gustava Poreba, who
    died on 8/31/1942 and who was born in Lewkowicz in 1899, is
    denied.

2. The Applicant will receive due to Article 24,25 BEG a sum
    of 2,466.66 German Marks for the time from 10/1/1939 to
    12/31/1948.

Translated in English, page two.

The Reason:

Based on Article 17 BEG, 7, the applicant is authorized to receive an Orphan pension until he is 16 years of age or until he has finished his education. Due to the fact that the father of the applicant was in a similar work situation (simple work) it is easy to classify the correct amount for the compensation. The accident pension is applied till 9/30/1951 in the amount of 2,067.00 German Marks, the orphan compensation is 51.67 per month and therefore 620 German Marks for the entire time. Due to the fact that the minimum pension is 100 German Marks, we have the following calculations from the 10/1/1939 till 12/31/1948, which marks the end of the applicant's education, we have the following calculation:

From 10/1/1939 till 2/28/1946

77 months X 100 R Marks = 7,700 Marks   1,540.00 German Marks

From 4/1/1947 till 6/20/1948
14 2/3 months X 100 RM = 1,466.67 Rm   293.33 German Marks

From 6/21/1948 till 12/31/1948
6 months X 100 German Marks   <u>633.33 German Marks</u>
                                        = 2,466.66 German Marks

In conclusion, the amount of 2,466.66 German Marks is awarded to the applicant as compensation.

In the case of compensation for the death of the mother, we regretfully deny compensation due to the fact that we can only pay compensation for one parent. As the period of death is longer for the father than the mother, we are paying the compensation for the father so the applicant will receive a higher amount.

To ensure the legality of this notice, please view the attached articles

In October 1988, Nathan filled out and mailed memorial pages of testimony for his parents and three sisters murdered in the Shoah. He sent the pages for inclusion in the Hall of Names at Yad Vashem World Holocaust Memorial Center in Jerusalem, Israel.

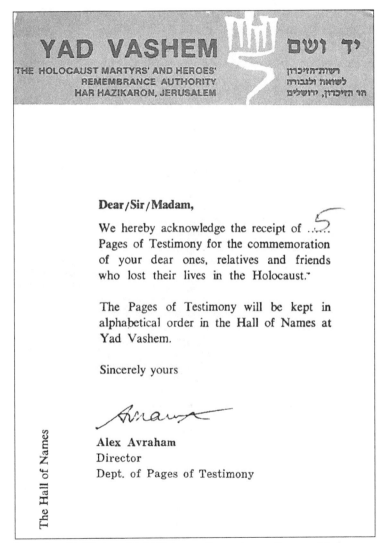

Letter from Yad Vashem World Holocaust Remembrance Center to Nathan Poremba, December 1988, acknowledging receipt of five Pages of Testimony memorializing his father, mother and three sisters murdered in the Holocaust.

Never Forget: Joseph, Gustava, Tala, Esta, and Sala Poremba individual "Pages of Testimony" are located in the "P" section of remembrance books at the Hall of Names, Yad Vashem World Holocaust Remembrance Center. (Photo by Joel Poremba, August 2018.)

CHAPTER TEN

THE REAL POLAND

POLAND'S LEGACY

What is Poland's identity in the aftermath of the Holocaust? What is its legacy regarding the Holocaust? What is the verdict on how Poles behaved before, during, and after the war? Who is Poland?

Over 7,000 men and women are recognized as "Polish Righteous Among the Nations," Poles listed as heroes at Yad Vashem for their actions in saving Jewish lives during the Holocaust. That number accounts for more than 25% of the more than 27,700 people recognized as "Righteous Among the Nations." Thus, Poles comprise the largest contingent within this elite group, honored and memorialized by Yad Vashem as people who risked their own lives to save Jews.[1] On the other hand, of the 3.3 million Jews who lived in Poland on the eve of World War II, less than 10% of them survived the Holocaust. It is estimated that 30,000 to 35,000 Polish Jews, or only 1% of all Polish Jewry, were saved with the help of Poles.[2]

One could argue Poles are the largest national group comprising the Righteous because most of the genocide took place in Poland. Perhaps this fact alone explains that a greater number of opportunities existed for Poles to save Jews. But, on the other hand, if 35,000 Jews were saved by Christian Poles and 7,112 individual Poles are counted as "Righteous

---

1. https://www.yadvashem.org/righteous/statistics.html, no author or year affixed.
2. https://www.yadvashem.org/righteous/stories/poland-historical-background.html, no author or year affixed.

Among the Nations," one could also argue this was merely because all the Nazi death camps were in Poland.

While this may be a cynical approach to explain why there are so many Righteous Poles listed at Yad Vashem, approximately 50,000 Jewish survivors were on Polish soil by the end of the Holocaust.[3] That number is shockingly dwarfed by the 3.3 million Jews that lived there before the Holocaust. But a deeper analysis of how Christian Poles acted during the Holocaust is required.

Many post-Holocaust scholarship has focused on the question of "who Poland was" during the Holocaust. Some works conclude Poland was helpful to its Jews because many of her citizens saved Jews. Others label Poland as less honorable because it conspired with the Nazis. Yet, others refer to Poland's pre-war and post-war anti-Jewish sentiment and antisemitic atmosphere.

But in this book, the answer to the question "who is Poland?" comes from a look into who witnessed pre-war Poland, the Holocaust, and post-war Poland. Nathan experienced both: those guided by genuine Christian compassion, and those who were violently anti-Jewish.

The Polish priest who sold Nathan's cousin, Leo, false papers for Nathan and Fela intended to help Jews. Without the priest's aid, Nathan and Fela would likely not have survived the Holocaust. The "Surdel" papers provided essential cover as Christian Poles. The priest took considerable risk in knowingly helping them to evade capture. The Polish priest was open to helping Leo and, in so doing, undoubtedly played a huge role in saving Nathan's and Fela's lives.

On the other hand, Nathan's Polish neighbors voluntarily accompanied the Germans on September 12, 1939, during the roundup of thirty-two Jewish men. They were happy to help the Nazis locate the Jews on the list. They did not do so for the German chocolate. They did it due to antisemitism. Nathan saw the look in the one Polish teen's eyes when he showed his disappointment that German troops failed to locate Joseph Poremba. He witnessed the Polish teen implore the German soldier to go back inside and search again. Later that day, Nathan also witnessed

---

3. Ibid.

Wieliczka Poles point and laugh and cavort while the Germans beat Jews who had been rounded up. On September 12, 1939, Nathan witnessed this before his father was taken to the forest and shot. A few weeks later, Poles gathered laughing while two Nazis assaulted and beat an orthodox Jew in Wieliczka.

The pre-war complicity between the Germans and the Wieliczka municipal clerk, a Pole, working undercover, is evidence of Polish complicity. This Pole compiled the list of Jews to be murdered in Wieliczka. At some point, the Polish municipal clerk, Mazurowski, simultaneously worked as city official while voluntarily working undercover as a spy for Germany. Nevertheless, on September 12, 1939, he was curiously helpful and participating with the SS officers in charge of the round-up, as witnessed by Nathan, his family, and the others.

There was also the open and obvious cooperation between the Nazis and Polish police who helped the former locate Jews. For example, in Wieliczka, on August 26, 1942, the deportation orders speak for themselves. The Polish police helped in the August 27, 1942, round up and deportation of Wieliczka Jews. Polish police also helped the Nazis block the city roads so no Jews could escape.

Had Joseph on the farm in Bibice known Nathan was Jewish, or any of the rural folk in the area known, they would have likely killed Nathan. Instead, Joseph specifically asked where Nathan was from and commented about Jews being from the cities, hoping he was not from a Polish city.

Had the drunken Polish bandit, perhaps associated with the Polish underground, known Nathan were Jewish, he too would have killed Nathan. After all, he bragged to Nathan about killing Jews.

There was the Polish woman and her family who took up residence in the Poremba home. She was not happy Nathan had survived the war, disappointed to see a Jew she knew from before the war. She had no qualms expressing how she felt seeing him. She refused even to allow him inside to retrieve personal items. Yet, another Polish neighbor acted with kindness and gave him a place to stay in her own home.

The Polish boys Nathan encountered after the war back home in Wieliczka illustrate the mood towards Jews after the genocide. They wanted to fight Nathan for no other reason than he was a Jew. The baseless animus they had for him was inexcusable.

Most significantly, there is also the fact local Poles tore down the memorial erected to the thirty-two martyrs in Wieliczka after the Holocaust. They were apparently either looking to whitewash the fact that Jews once lived in Wieliczka or that Wieliczka Poles were involved in their murder or both. It is quite telling that Wieliczka, a once-proud Jewish community, saw fit to re-write this part of its history. Perhaps the monument's removal served both purposes: pretending no Jews had lived there and erasing its complicity with the Nazis.

Poland continues to deal with the complexities of its wartime history. In January 2018, the Polish government criminalized (with jail time and a fine) the accusation of Polish collaboration with the Nazis. This law was passed in both houses of Poland's parliament. In February 2018, then-Polish President Andrzej Duda signed the bill into law. But after much international debate, Poland amended the law, decriminalizing discussion of Polish complicity. But the qualifying condition on decriminalizing the law pertained to only when a person said it "commits such an act as part of artistic or scientific activities." [4]

Poland's Law and Justice government subsequently acknowledged that individual Poles did take part in crimes against Polish Jews but also took the position that the newly amended Holocaust law was still moral and "correct" because the Polish state ceased to exist under Nazi occupation.[5] Eighty years earlier, the Polish government, both in Warsaw and at the state and local institution levels, issued anti-Semitic laws during the Holocaust.[6] But not much has changed over that time, given the semantic games Poland engaged in meant to further whitewash Poland's ugly wartime history.

---

4. https://www.bbc.com/news/world-europe-44627129, no author, June 27, 2018.

5. Adam Easton, *Why has Poland backtracked on Holocaust law?* https://www.bbc.com/news/world-europe-44627129, June 27, 2018.

6. Robert Michael, *Holy Hatred: Christianity, Antisemitism, and the Holocaust* (Palgrave MacMillan, 2006), 178.

The shameful and ongoing whitewashing of Polish history continues. The embarrassing wordsmithing that no law has been broken as long as it is made in the academic setting is juvenile. The excuse that Poland could not possibly have helped the Nazis because its government was in ruins and eliminated by the Nazi takeover is equally disappointing. Its post-war failure to take responsibility for its conduct with the German army, both Polish government officials and Polish citizens, is well documented.

CHAPTER ELEVEN

THE LAST JEW OF WIELICZKA

THE SURVIVOR'S DUTY

Nathan is most likely the last Jewish survivor of the Shoah from Wieliczka, Poland. He is now 91 years young. The few Jews who returned to Wieliczka after the war in 1945 were between thirty and forty years older than Nathan. He was only fifteen at that time and was perhaps the youngest Jewish survivor from Wieliczka. Therefore, it is likely the case he is the last Jew of Wieliczka.

Fela, who also survived, eventually moved from New York to Los Angeles with Nathan. She died in 1961 at the age of thirty-two. She married and had one son, Joseph, and one daughter, Barbara.

Of the 3.3 million Jews who called Poland home in 1939, about 90% died during the war. The Germans and their Polish accomplices murdered the overwhelming majority. In addition, some Polish Jews were killed by their own countrymen.

Nathan moved from New York to Los Angeles in 1960. He married Irene in 1966 and had two sons, Joel and Alan. The "J" Nathan chose to take in memory of his father, Joseph. He gave it to his first-born son, the author of this book. The author, together with his wife, Sari, have two children, Noah and Gabi. The "N" for Noah was given in memory of Natalie Poremba, Talia or Tala, Nathan's sister. The "G" was given for Gabi in memory of Nathan's mother, Gustava. Through the author, Noah and Gabi, the memories of those who perished lives on.

The improbable six-year survival of a nine-year-old Jewish boy is a remarkable story of resistance. There were dozens of incidents that could have resulted in his death, but none did. While luck had a role, so too did the examples of courage from his parents. His father taught him to stand up to antisemitism. His mother provided him the freedom to move and the opportunity to fight for his life in the manner he saw fit.

When he was being bullied in school at an early age, Nathan found a creative way to end the torment by paying a bigger boy to protect him. As a result, he saw his father confront antisemitism before the Holocaust, and Nathan learned from his example.

After his father's murder, Nathan risked death by choosing not to wear the required Star of David armband. Certainly, he did it in defiance of the law, but he also did it to sustain his family by getting desperately needed food. These acts set him on a path wherein he refused to acquiesce to his own death and instead dared to keep living and fighting for survival.

What are the responsibilities of a Holocaust survivor? To bear witness and educate, many would agree. But what has prompted the duty when the survivor undertakes the task of giving his or her testimony? To put the answer in context, consider Auschwitz survivor Primo Levi's paraphrased quote from Simon Wiesenthal, Nazi hunter and survivor of the Janowska, Płaszów, and Gross-Rosen concentration camps:

> However this war may end, we have won the war against you; none of you will be left to bear witness, but even if some of you survive, the world would not believe him. There will perhaps be suspicions, discussions, research by historians, but there will be no certainties because we will destroy the evidence together with you. And even if some proof should remain and some of you survive, people will say that the events you describe are too monstrous to be believed: they will say they are the exaggerations of Allied propaganda and will believe us, who will deny everything,

and not you. We will be the ones to dictate the history of the Lagers. —SS Officer [1]

Simon Wiesenthal remembered that SS militiamen enjoyed cynically admonishing camp prisoners with the notion that no one would believe the horrors survivors of the Holocaust endured. This is the duty the survivor embraces when he or she comes forward to tell his or her story. While Nathan never read either Levi or Wiesenthal, he repeated the same paraphrased quote for decades. He re-stated it often to his sons to encourage at least one of them to help tell his story.

Ironically, while Nathan embodied evidence of resilience and adaptive ability, tenaciousness, and self-awareness for six long years of war, he could not replicate this afterward. Even while blessed with those strengths, he struggled to tell his survival story. While safe in New York City and Los Angeles after the war, Nathan's emotional scars ran deep. They caused him to overcompensate when it came to shelter and food. Without the consistency of either one during the war, that complex he carried afterward never fully evaporated. The constant fear of not having a proper roof over his head, warm clothes, and enough food followed him his entire adult life in America despite never lacking for them. The story of the Holocaust is how a person copes in the worst environment. In the direst human situation imaginable, Nathan's experience, an extreme reality that has no parallel in modern history, still battles to maintaining his humanity every day. These are some of the consequences of having survived the Holocaust.

Over the next fifty years, Nathan watched the world fix its attention on the Holocaust, but something always bothered him in that respect. He watched the 1961 trial of Adolf Eichmann. He heard academics discuss Anne Frank's *The Diary of a Young Girl*, watched the American television series *Holocaust*, *Escape from Sobibor*, and *Conspiracy*. He went to the theater to see the films like *Schindler's List* and *The Pianist*. But these

---

1. Primo Levi, *The Drowned and the Saved*, R. Rosenthal (trans.) (New York: Vintage International, 1989), 11–12; paraphrasing Simon Wiesenthal, *The Murderers Are Among Us*, J. Wechsberg (ed.), (Columbus, OH; McGraw-Hill, 1967).

big box productions and hand-picked news events focused solely on the Nazi Final Solution, concentration and death camps, and ghettos. Few media depictions, if any, focused on the experience of flight survivors like Nathan. Despite the fact they were the largest group of Jews to outlast the Nazi regime, numbering in the hundreds of thousands, their stories are not often told.

Nathan was always modestly uncomfortable with the quality of the narrative about the Holocaust when, as he said, "Most of us survived the way I did." This was his way of saying he wanted to tell his story but also did not know how. So what was the obstacle in telling of his experiences?

Like most survivors, Nathan suppressed his experiences for fifty-three years before opening up to the Shoah Foundation in October 1998. The path he took to get to that point was not easily reached. Over that half-century, Nathan was no different than other survivors who repressed their experiences during the war to protect their children from their past. By doing this, Nathan passed the delayed mourning to his own children. While lighting annual *yahrzeit* candles (memory candles) for his family to commemorate the anniversary of their deaths, Nathan navigated any discussion of his experiences away from his sons. The suppressed trauma he sustained during the Holocaust, pushing it to the back of his mind, acted to distance himself from the terror while trying to embrace a new life.

The emotional baggage of the Holocaust survivor is not easily shed. Guilt or "survivor syndrome" did not end the moment Nathan set foot in New York in May 1951. He often asked himself, "Why did I survive?" and it weighed on him his entire life. The struggle to move on with his own life while his family was left behind was not so easily cured. Nathan would spend the next five decades experiencing nightmares, intrusive memories, and flashbacks of his life during the war. Nightmares include having to run for his life from Nazis, struggling to ensure he was properly hidden from the authorities, and worse, being caught by German soldiers. These are additional consequences of surviving the war. The nightmares were something that never abated with time. Another effect of having survived is the shame over being a victim and the fear of being stigmatized by being one. When something bad happens to people, there is often the feeling that the person did something wrong to have deserved it. Not always the case, Nathan blamed himself for his experiences, citing his decision to run away from his mother in 1942 as the reason he had endured such hardship for three long years.

In the end, Nathan re-established a sense of control that was absent for six years during the war. He was able to realize a sense of safety in recognized routines. He worked seven days a week in two convenience stores he owned with another survivor. Even though he could afford a home cleaning service, a landscaper, pool service, and automatic car wash, he would spend the next fifty years undertaking these tasks himself (and later entrusting his two sons to it). What modern American fathers took for granted, Nathan did not. He preferred doing with his hands and having the freedom to work with deadlines without help from contractors. This, too, was a consequence of being a survivor.

The Shoah survivors are among the most inspiring people
I have had the privilege to meet. Remarkably, despite
coming eyeball to eyeball with the angel of death,
despite the unimaginable losses each of them suffered,
so many of them fulfilled the words of Moses' great
command 'uvacharta bachayim,' 'choose life.' In doing so,
they chose life not just for themselves, but for their children,
grandchildren, and all future generations."
—Rabbi Lord Jonathan Sacks, z"l

Joel and Nathan Poremba, October 26, 1996.

EPILOGUE

MY EARLY RECOGNITION OF THE HOLOCAUST

At a young age, maybe five or six, I was aware that millions of Jews had been murdered in Europe during the Holocaust. I knew my father survived it and that he lost both his parents and three sisters. I was aware half of those slaughtered in the Shoah were Polish Jews. We had two pre-war photos of the father's family framed and displayed in our home. I spent hours gazing at the photos looking for answers. I wanted the photos to speak to me, but they would not tell me much of anything. The photos could not explain to me how it was my father made it through the war but his parents and three sisters had not.

When I was little, my father's Polish survivor friends often visited our home. I remember visiting with them. I saw numbered tattoos on their forearms. My father would proudly point to one of them and tell me, "She survived Auschwitz-Birkenau," and introduce me to another "He survived Płaszów," and "These two here, they escaped from Majdanek." They would proceed to list the numerous ghettos they were put or hid in: the Warsaw, Kraków, Łódź, Radom, Tarnów, Lwów. I was not even ten years old, but I seemed to know more about other survivors than I did about my own father. They all survived, but none of them discussed how. It was clear the emotional blocks my father exhibited were more common than I understood.

I saw my father's survivor friends as heroes and all-stars. For me, they were bigger than the Honus Wagners, Ty Cobbs, Babe Ruths, and Sandy Koufaxes of the baseball world. Polish Jews who survived were larger than life to me because they had been persecuted, that lost their families, and had been hunted by an unrelenting killing machine.

I scoured their faces for the secrets and stories that might explain how they survived. Why did their faces not tell their stories? Why did my father's face not tell his story? I never found it on their faces. It was never going to be that easy. It was going to take much more effort.

I attended a Hebrew day school in Los Angeles, Kadima Hebrew Academy, from kindergarten through sixth grade. After that, I went to Herzl Schools from seventh through ninth grade. I distinctly remember the outbreak of the Yom Kippur War in October 1973 and my first grade Hebrew teacher, an Israeli, talking about the many "elimination wars" Israel had faced since its statehood in 1948. In that same conversation, she mentioned the Holocaust, which preceded Israel's independence. She commented how all Israeli wars to date had been defensive wars that had to be fought just to exist. This tiny bit of information functioned as a bridge to what little I had been exposed to at home.

My teacher was asking: "When will the world leave us alone?" That point stuck with me early on.

Guilt as a "Second Generation"

Without the Holocaust, it is quite likely I would never have been born. The odds my father would have ever left Jewish Poland are next to zero without the Shoah having happened.

Pre-war Kraków was affectionately known as "Jerusalem-North" for hundreds of years before the founding of the State of Israel. What Polish Jews would have left for America in 1810? 1910? 1930? My grandfather had almost two hundred family members living in and around Jewish Kraków. My grandmother's family numbered in the dozens in the same area. Arguably Southern Poland was fertile Jewish real estate even if it was the frozen tundra half of the year.

The Nuremberg Laws came to Germany in 1935, the war then came to Poland in 1939, and it was too late for my family to have left Poland. By the time the Final Solution came to Europe in 1942, my father's parents and three out of four sisters had all been murdered by the Nazis.

Over two hundred members of his family members had been slain. But my father survived it, but predictably this is why my father left Poland and Europe altogether. The country, and arguably the continent, was no longer home to most of the world's Jews.

I owe my life to my father leaving Poland due to the Holocaust. Without it, my father would never have had cause to emigrate to the United States, where he met my mother and built a Jewish life. None of this happens without his family being wiped out. This has been difficult for me to reconcile.

But then I met four special men on the 2018 Momentum trip to Israel. Each of them gave me something invaluable that permitted me to get above the noise and face it.

I came to learn that my father lived as a hero from 1939 through 1945. He fought to live, and he resisted his tormentors, both Nazis and Poles alike. He fought for every minute of his life during a war that seemed without end. To do so not only took tremendous strength and commitment but hope in the face of horror and courage under the threat of death which hovered over him nearly every minute of every day for six years.

My father thrived by creating a Jewish life after the war, marrying a Jewish woman, and educating his two Jewish sons in Hebrew day schools. In addition, he bar mitzvahed both his sons and attended both grandchildren's bar and bat mitzvahs, racking up four *aliyot* (called to the Torah) at these *simchas* (Jewish celebration).

This was more than surviving. It was thriving. His bearing witness and testimony fulfill Elie Wiesel's notion of duty.

PURSUIT OF MY FATHER AND HIS SHOAH STORY

I spent the first thirty-one years of my life seeking to understand how my father survived the Holocaust as a boy in Poland. By the time he was nine years old, Nathan had lost his father, who the Nazis had murdered. At age eleven, he told his mother he wanted to run away from his Nazi-occupied town, Wieliczka. He did not feel safe in his town, which was under threat of imminent deportation orders. So he boldly said goodbye to his mother and three sisters and went on the run.

A Jewish child this young in occupied German territory in 1942 was marked for death. That is, of course, if he were caught. So how did my father evade the Nazis for six long years?

I did not know because I was never told. My father simply did not want to talk about it. Most of the time, my father did not want to answer questions about his life in Poland. He did not want to burden people with what he went through as a child.

As I was growing up, my father made comments here and there about the Holocaust. Truly little of what he discussed was personal. Whenever he found me watching a Holocaust documentary on television, he would usually leave the room or change the subject if I attempted to enter his past. I discovered if I asked general questions about Poland or the Nazis, he might talk a little, but if I asked him specifically about how he survived or how his family perished, he would turn the conversation in another direction.

I wanted to know what he went through. How did he make it through the war alone, with both parents murdered by 1942? How did he find shelter, food, and water for six years, knowing that at any moment, he could be discovered, captured, and executed? How did he live under the pressure of knowing his life could end at any time?

My father is a quiet man, reserved, restrained, and unassuming. He is not one to talk about himself, his troubles, worries, or misfortunes. He rarely expresses emotion. To meet him, one would never know the horrors he survived and witnessed. As a result, I chased my dad around for thirty-one years, pressing him for his story. But the response was usually silence.

To fill the hole of not knowing, I immersed myself in the facts and stories of the Holocaust. If I could not get information from my father, I would try to obtain it from the stories of others. I read many survivor stories and memoirs. I memorized Eastern European town names, large and small. I learned about the pre- and post-war Jewish populations of various European countries. I studied the locations of Nazi slaughters in and outside of death camps. I kept track of how many shuls and Jewish businesses existed in various towns before the war. As if that was not enough, I watched hundreds of hours of documentaries on the Holocaust and World War II; read dozens of books written by academics; attended dozens of presentations and lectures given by survivors. I took a handful of college courses on the Holocaust. I even watched the renowned ten-hour subtitled documentary, *Shoah*, by Claude Lanzmann. Twice. I wanted to learn and try to feel what survivors had felt, but I discovered I was filling holes with all the wrong items over time. Absorbing this knowledge left me with indescribable sadness. It led to anger rather than understanding, helplessness rather than relatability, and inevitably made me feel like a victim.

This was not a productive path for the son of a survivor to walk or anyone else for that matter. Worse, these were not emotions my father wanted for the members of his family. On the contrary, they were the very ones he guarded against by not sharing his story. I understood this, but at the same time, since he would not discuss his survival, I believed all I could do was bury myself in the tragedies of the Jewish people during the Shoah as a substitute.

I impaired myself in the sadness as a method to better understand. I thought this was the essence of my father's story. I wanted to feel the despair and the horror, to touch it as best I could. I assumed all along that every story I read had to be a version of what my father had experienced.

THE EFFECT OF *SCHINDLER'S LIST* AND THE SHOAH FOUNDATION ON MY FATHER

Fast forward to December 1993, the movie *Schindler's List* was released. I saw the movie the first time with my father, mother, and brother in a local theater. Three of us left crying and upset, but not my father. For the first time, he shared something of his experiences as we left the theater. He sought to draw a connection between the film and his own survival. In a rare glimpse into his life, he touched on two things: first, he said the film accurately depicted what went on in the labor camp, Płaszów, a camp prominently depicted in the movie. He mentioned family who were killed there, a few friends who survived there, and his own brief stay there. The second thing he shared was more personal. He said that when he was in the Kraków Ghetto, he sneaked in and out under the cover and commotion provided by the approximately 1,200 Jews as they went to and from Oskar Schindler's nearby enamel factory. At the time, he had no idea who this group was, where they were going, or why, but said he used their entries and exits as an opportunity to get in and out of the ghetto safely.

For the first time, it appeared my dad wanted to talk about the Holocaust, and more specifically, about the details of his own story. But alas, it was short-lived. He was not yet ready for it. In the aftermath of the movie, he still refused to speak about his survival.

The movie's success created a dialogue around the world about preserving Holocaust survivors' stories. This developed into the creation of the Shoah Foundation in 1994 (since becoming the USC Shoah Foundation for Visual History and Education in 2006). The Foundation's goal is to do audio-visual interviews with survivors and witnesses of the Holocaust before they are no longer with us. To set this up, one had merely to call the Foundation, book an interviewer/videographer team to come to one's home, and they would record testimony. But my dad was not interested.

None of my father's local survivor friends, all from Poland, living and working in Los Angeles, wanted to be interviewed either.

What the movie did for me was to change my perspective about my father. He was no longer just a "survivor." He was a hero. Every other documentary and movie I had watched was not personal, so when I learned about this survivor or that one, it was easy to fall into the trap of treating the subject merely as an academic exercise.

But my father had done something new, small though it was. He had woven a link from his life to the movie. It was a fleeting moment, but what little he shared awakened something. He was not just a "survivor," meaning "to get by" or "to do just enough," he was a witness. He did much more than that, I could tell. Certainly, the movie portrayed the "Schindler Jews" doing much more than "just making it through."

That unique group persevered, yes, but after the Holocaust, there was much more to them than just being survivors. They did much more than that, they thrived.

It occurred to me, so too did my father.

S T E V E N   S P I E L B E R G

April 29, 2004

Dear Nathan,

I am thrilled to tell you that 2004 marks the 10th anniversary of Survivors of the Shoah Visual History Foundation. These have been exciting, productive, and wondrous years. In 1994, I could not fully foresee the power, impact, and success of this massive archive, or how your testimony and the 52,000 others we have collected would ultimately affect those who watch them. But survivors convinced me that their stories, your story, had to be told.

Today, I am honored to tell you that young people and adults are watching your testimonies in schools, libraries, museums, and universities—not only in the United States, but in countries around the world. Through documentaries, special collections, educational products and programs, and as research tools for scholars and researchers, your testimonies are making a profound difference by creating a bridge between history and contemporary issues.

It is thanks to you, and your willingness to recall, retell, and record testimony, that all this is possible. The archive will serve as a valuable resource not only for countless people today, but for future generations. It is through your generosity that children 100 years from now and beyond will hear and learn about the terrible consequences of hatred and racism. By hearing your voice and seeing your face, they will recognize that they have the power to bring about change and act against intolerance.

I want to thank you so very much for your priceless contribution to the Shoah Foundation archive. You are helping us to achieve our urgent mission to overcome prejudice, intolerance, and bigotry — and the suffering they cause — through the educational use of the Foundation's visual history testimonies.

I am proud of what we have accomplished together, and you have made it possible. I thank you for your priceless gift.

All my best,

Steven

SURVIVORS OF THE SHOAH VISUAL HISTORY FOUNDATION · POST OFFICE BOX 3168 · LOS ANGELES, CA 90078-3168

Letter from Steven Spielberg, Shoah Visual History Foundation, April 29, 2004.

As the Shoah Foundation booked hundreds of interviews which became thousands, my father's survivor friends slowly began one by one, to book their own Foundation interviews. Over time, all of them gave their testimonies except my father. He was still not ready to share.

In 1998, my wife and I were expecting our first child. By that time, I had spent four years begging my dad to sit for the Foundation interview. I then challenged him: "Can you give your testimony before your first grandchild is born?" He said "No." But at our son, Noah's, *brit milah* (Hebrew for "covenant circumcision"), my father approached me and said he would give his testimony to the Foundation.

My wife and I were in my parents' home the day he gave his testimony October 4, 1998. For almost four hours, he spoke, he wept, and he testified. We were at one end of the house, and the interview was at the other end. I knew it would be difficult for my father to sit and open up if I was there. A few times, I eavesdropped on some of the interview. What little I heard shattered me. The pain I heard and felt from his cadence pierced through and paralyzed me. Finally, I walked away as I could not bear to hear any more of it.

I had heard my father cry only once before, and that was at my bar mitzvah when the rabbi of our shul blessed me on the *bima*. Before the rabbi recited the *birkat hakohanim*, Rabbi Eli Schochet referred to my father's Shoah survival. Then, the Rabbi pointed to the back of the synagogue at the *yahrzeit* plaques displaying the names of my father's family who died in the Shoah. That was the first time I saw him fight back the tears.

These tears reflected loss. But the tears I heard during my father's Shoah Foundation interview were much different. Those were tears of suffering, torture, and indescribable sadness.

The interview caused my dad to relive the pain, desperation, loss, and fear. But this pain was inflicted by human beings. His tears reflected humankind's indifference. I could not listen to it. I then retreated altogether from wanting to hear my father's story. All the horrors of the Holocaust I had absorbed up until then were nothing compared to listening to my father's own experiences. It made the Holocaust more real, almost too real.

The shoe was now on the other foot. The Shoah Foundation interview freed my father because it was therapeutic and liberating for him. He was no longer afraid to talk about his life during the Holocaust. Now he wanted to share it. He now chased me around, begging me to sit down and listen. But all I could do was run from him.

It would be another twenty-two years before I could broach the subject. It took me this long to watch my father's Shoah Foundation interview; and to sit down and talk with him about his survival face-to-face.

It would take an experience of a lifetime of my own to turn me around.

I owe this to not only going to Israel for the very first time but doing it with a unique program helmed by a founder who staffed the trip with amazing Jewish people.

Trip to Israel with "Momentum Men"

In 2018, the opportunity arrived for me to make my first visit to Israel. Through the Jewish Women's Renaissance Project, "Momentum Men" was created to provide Jewish husbands an experience to look into their Jewish soul while doing so in Israel. The rich and meaningful program was enhanced by its trip leaders, guest lecturers, and local leaders who accompanied the men. The program is demonstrative and instructive on how to be better fathers and husbands, with Torah as the center and root of our lives. This is Founding Director Lori Palatnik's vision in connecting Jewish families living in the Diaspora to Israel.

The trip was the catalyst that unlocked what I had been hiding for too long. It provided the push I needed to open up to my father. One could say that Momentum was created to bolster the Jewish family and to create a bridge between the Diaspora and Israel, and that is certainly true, but the program's underlying theme is to "choose awesome" Momentum showed me how to be mindful of where I was coming from and how to get where I wanted to go with these complex feelings. It rearranged my perspective about the Holocaust and offered me an approach I had not been exposed to.

The 2018 Momentum Israel men's trip was led by Saul Blinkoff. He provided dozens of insights converged through universally applicable real-life stories. But, for me, two of Saul's thoughts stood above all the others. The first was to "get busy living or get busy dying."

Most of us have heard this line. This statement hit me from the minute he said it. It made sense to me because for far too long, I had dwelled on what world Jewry had lost in the Holocaust instead of focusing on the gains we have made despite it.

On the Israel trip, Saul, a former Disney animator/director, motivational speaker, producer at DreamWorks Animation, and podcast host of the inspirational weekly podcast, "Life of AWESOME!" did much more than state the line. He showed our group how it worked. He stressed that an active Jewish life is the answer to questions about our people's tragic past. Judaism, he said, is the baseball bat to take to the horrors of persecution and genocide. We should use Torah's lessons to brush away the past and push forward. We were not built to live in sadness because of tragedy, Saul said. Torah, he said, contained the roadmap for dealing with tragedy and encouraged us to not just "be" Jewish but to "live" Jewish. Hanging one's head in defeat, he said, was not living. The six million did not perish for us to be sad. Instead, I realized they wanted us to live a life they were prevented from living, a life of meaning. Saul explained that through Torah, we have the opportunity to take halachic wisdom from our past and do something good with it. One does not absorb the horrors of persecution and wallow in it. Instead, he explained, one can make something consequential with his/her life.

We were created by G-d to use Torah to build a home. We were not created to cry over the one destroyed. He was right.

As I approached the Kotel for my first time after being at Yad Vashem earlier that day, Saul reminded us all to "turn pain into purpose." This was the second message from Saul that resonated with me. This was my pivot.

I internalized much as a member of the Second Generation. I have not known how to move past the emotions I kept inside. Saul's message functioned as a ladder, and I decided I needed to grab on to it and climb out. I was compelled to end the emotional paralysis and turn the page. Saul said we did not go to Yad Vashem earlier in the day to follow it up with a walk to the Kotel to be sad. We took that walk to remind ourselves to embrace our Jewish identity and challenge ourselves how to utilize that identity every day of our lives to serve humanity. Torah gives us the example of how to live. It is filled with instances of our forebearers turning pain and tragedy into meaning and purpose. Saul kept reminding our group that living and rejoicing in Israel was the ultimate "We're still here. Our Torah is still here, G-d's light is still here".

My father did this, but I had been blind to it. My father had a story of resistance to tell, and it needed to be heard by his son at long last.

Yaakov Selavan, a former IDF tank captain, made the same point. At Latrun, Israel, Captain Selavan said:

> . . . did people die so we could sit all day and cry and do nothing with our lives? The answer is 'no.' They [IDF defensive war soldiers] died so we could be here and live a meaningful life. Our mission now is to make this price worth it.

Captain Selavan was referencing Israeli armored corps members whose names are memorialized on walls outside the Latrun museum, Yad La-Shiryon Latrun. They did not die for us to be sad. They died so we could live and do something *with* life.

This applied to me when I thought about the Shoah and my father's family who perished. Those who died in the Shoah died so that the rest of us could live. The Warsaw Uprising, the resistance to the Nazi war machine, inspired an entire future and taught Israel to defend herself no matter what tragedy happened yesterday.

The Momentum trip woke me up from a long sleep. Before it, I treaded water in the darkness of the Holocaust. I assumed feeling the horror was the way to learn about it. The trip's leaders showed this was not true. This was not what my father's family died for. Sadness is not what six million Jews died for.

Another speaker, Charlie Harary, whose grandfather was a Holocaust survivor, spoke about the art of "the crossover," the dribble exhibited by basketball players. He told us that the ability to move one way, to sell it to an adversary convincingly, and to immediately shift one's momentum the other way, and do that convincingly, was the magic in the soup of life.

But what did his grandfather's survival have to do with a basketball move? Charlie's explanation went like this:

One day Charlie's grandfather was sharing his survival story with him. They were both brought to tears discussing the Shoah. Charlie was not finished processing the emotions he was feeling, and neither was his grandfather, but suddenly they were interrupted. Charlie's son was on the floor playing with a Lego set and interrupted them requesting his great grandfather help build the set. Without missing a beat, Charlie's grandfather wiped the tears from his face and pivoted to the floor to build and play with his great-grandson. He left the sorrow and moved instantly to his great-grandchild. How did he do this without needing a moment?

The point is this: wherever you are in life, that is where you need to be 100%. His grandfather was fully in the moment telling Charlie about his experiences during the Holocaust, but he was adept to switch immediately and pivot when his great-grandson asked him to play with him.

To be successful in life, one needs to be able to master the art of the crossover, to learn how to pivot in a snap, to be able to turn from immeasurable sadness to the joys that life brings.

Charlie's message was clear: remember the horrors of the Holocaust, yes, but when called upon, be available to live life to the fullest without suffering the past.

On the same trip was City Leader Rabbi Yisroel Ciner, my rabbi and group leader from Orange County, California. His guidance and support while discussing all these issues were effortless on his part and yielded much for me to think about.

He asked why I chose to go on the trip. I told him I was looking to get out from under the weight of the Holocaust and that I was in search of a spark to be able to connect with my father, to have the strength to sit down with him, hear about his life and move forward.

I told Rabbi Ciner that I had held onto my father's Shoah Foundation video for too long and had not the strength to watch it. I told the Rabbi of the guilt I bore as a Second Generation, that I had carried it around my entire life. Rabbi Ciner said, "You are a product of his triumph, not his tragedies."

I realized I am not here because the Holocaust happened, something I had always burdened myself with. Instead, I am here because of what my father overcame.

Standing before the Kotel for the very first time, a small part of me was afraid of what I might feel and see. Was I going to express anger at G-d because of the Shoah? Was I going to be mindful and recite the mourner's kaddish for my father's family? Was I going to be humble and thank G-d for the life He bestowed on me? I did not know what I was going to feel. I carried with me the weight of notes written by my family and those I wrote to place in cracks in the Kotel Wall.

The words I wrote about my father's family echoed over and over in my head. I inserted notes into the Walls' cracks, instinctively put my talis and tefillin on, closed my eyes, and said the *Shema*. Instead of anger or sadness, I felt warmth. I felt protected, and I felt free. I felt privileged to stand there and acknowledge G-d and those who came before me, those who died so I could be standing there.

For the first time in my life, I took a step forward about the Shoah. There was no need to weep over it as I had. I had been given keys to pivot so that by the time I stood before G-d at the Wall, I knew what to do.

When I left the Kotel, I knew upon my return home that I would have the strength to sit down with my father and learn of the horrors and triumphs that comprise the puzzle of his life's story. The trip's inspiration, "It's not WHAT you know, it's what you DO with what you know," said it best. We must act.

AFTERWORD

Resistance takes many forms. In the years closer to the devastation of the Holocaust, it was the Warsaw Ghetto uprising or the escape from Sobibor that captured the imagination and pride of the Jewish world. With the more nuanced perspective that can only be gained from a greater distance as the years have passed, different types of resistance are now recognized, valued, and honored. The idea of spiritual resistance, maintaining one's faith, one's humanity, one's drive to help others, one's self-dignity while being treated as a subhuman has been recognized as being truly heroic.

My dear friend, Joel Poremba, has done the world a great service by sharing with us the true heroism of his father, Nathan Poremba. As a young boy growing up in a Polish city that was virulently antisemitic well before Nazi arrival, Nathan learned the skills necessary that led to his unique form of resistance. He watched his father Joseph stand up to antisemites, using his physical stature and strength when necessary, to take down antisemitic banners and placards and even to take down a champion Polish wrestler. But he also witnessed his father's polite, fair-mindedness, who, through his choice of words and manner, had the ability to diffuse tense and volatile situations.

As a small, frail six-year-old, Nathan found himself the only Jewish child in that city's public school system. Facing physical assault from the other children sanctioned and encouraged by the emotional abuse of the teachers who proclaimed that Jews must sit in the back of the class, Nathan honed the survival skills of his heroic resistance. Then, using his candy money, he *hired* his greatest tormentor to serve as his protector at six years old.

Joel not only relates his father's story but brings us into the mind, heart, and soul of his father, Nathan Poremba, as he survives for six years as an orphaned nine-year-old amid a world of horror consumed by unbridled hate.

Nathan Poremba's heroic resistance consists of refusal to give up or give in. Of living. Of persevering. Of surviving against all odds and ultimately thriving and granting grandchildren to his murdered parents and extended family.

The banners in his city and across Poland read: Jews out of Poland. Jews go back to Palestine. One contrasts that with today's calls of Jews go back to Poland; Jews get out of Palestine. At times it seems that the world grants no place at all for us Jews. It is in this context that the heroic resistance of Nathan Poremba stands out.

We will not succumb, we will not give up or give in, we will persevere, we will thrive. Following in the path of Nathan Poremba, Am Yisrael Chai, the Jewish Nation is *alive*!

Thank you, Nathan, and thank you, Joel, for sharing his life and lessons with us.

Rabbi Yisroel Ciner
Beth Jacob Congregation of Irvine
https://www.bethjacobirvine.org/

END NOTES

CHAPTER ONE: A JEWISH CITY IN THE SHADOW OF KRAKÓW

1. Shmuel Meiri (ed.), *The Jewish Community of Wieliczka; A Memorial Book, (Kehilat Wieliczka; Sefer Zikaron)*, (The Wieliczka Assoc. in Israel, M. Stern Press, 1980), [English version], 7.
2. Ibid., 20.
3. Ibid., 36.
4. Shmuel Spector, Geoffrey, Wigoder (eds.), *The Encyclopedia of Jewish Life Before and During the Holocaust*, (NYU Press, 2001), 1442; Michael Berenbaum, Fred Skolnik (eds.), *Encyclopaedia Judaica*, (Macmillan Reference USA in association with the Keter Pub. House, 2007), Volume 16, 242, 496.
5. ChaeRan Freez, Paula E. Hyman, Antony Polonsky (eds.), *Polin; Studies in Polish Jewry*, (Liverpool University Press., Littman Library of Jewish Civilization, 2007), Volume 18, 193, fn 15.
6. Megargee, Geoffrey (2012). *The United States Holocaust Memorial Museum Encyclopedia of Camps and Ghettos 1933-1945*, ["USHMM"], (Bloomington, Indiana: University of Indiana Press), Volume II, 591. https://www.belzec.eu/en/page/deportations/238
7. https://sztetl.org.pl/en/towns/w/322-wieliczka/99-history/138230-history-of-community
8. Spector, *The Encyclopedia of Jewish Life Before and During the Holocaust*, 1442.
9. William W. Hagen, *Anti-Jewish Violence in Poland, 1914-1920*, (Cambridge University Press, 2018), 102–108.
10. Richard J. Evans, *The Third Reich at War*, (Penguin Press, 2010), 49.
11. Meiri, *The Jewish Community of Wieliczka*, 9–10.
12. Rafal Pankowski, *The Populist Radical Right in Poland: The Patriots* (Routledge, 2010), 26.
13. Roman Dmowski, *Polityka Polska i odbudowanie państwa* ("Polish Politics and the Rebuilding of the State"), (1925), 301–308.
14. Gunnar Paulsson, *Secret City: The Hidden Jews of Warsaw*, 1940–1945 (Yale University Press, 2002), 38.
15. Andrzej Walicki, *The Troubling Legacy of Roman Dmowski*, East European Politics & Societies (December 1999, vol. 14), 28–29.
16. Meiri, *The Jewish Community of Wieliczka*, 29–32.

CHAPTER TWO: ANTISEMITISM IN WIELICZKA, 1935–1939

1. Norman Goda, *The Holocaust: Europe, the World, and the Jews, 1918–1945* (Taylor & Francis, 2012), 73–74.

CHAPTER THREE: A LION OF JUDAH: A FATHER'S FEARLESS LEADERSHIP

[none]

CHAPTER FOUR: THE SHOAH DESCENDS UPON WIELICZKA

1. Meiri, *The Jewish Community of Wieliczka*, 36.
2. Evans, *The Third Reich at War*, 318.
3. Meiri, *The Jewish Community of Wieliczka*, 36.
4. Jan Grabowski, *Hunt for the Jews* (Indiana University Press, 2013), 101–120.
5. Ibid., 103–104.
6. Ofer Aderet, 'Orgy of Murder': The Poles Who 'Hunted" Jews and Turned Them Over to The Nazis, https://www.haaretz.com/world-news/.premium.MAGAZINE-orgy-of-murder-the-poles-who-hunted-jews-and-turned-them-in-1.5430977, (Haaretz.com, 2017).
7. Meiri, *The Jewish Community of Wieliczka*, 36.
8. Ibid., 37.
9. Ibid., 37–38.
10. Józef ("Yossek") Bakalarz, Nathan Poremba's first cousin and an Auschwitz sonderkommando survivor, visited Wieliczka in 1995, verified the monument and name plates memorializing the thirty-two Jewish men murdered on September 12, 1939 had been removed after the Holocaust by resident Wieliczka Poles, not by Soviet officials.
11. Megargee, *USHMM Encyclopedia of Camps and Ghettos*, Vol. 2, 591–592.
12. Meiri, *The Jewish Community of Wieliczka*, 40.
13. Ibid., 47.

CHAPTER FIVE: A WOMAN OF VALOR: A MOTHER'S SACRIFICE TO SAVE HER CHILDREN

1. Megargee, *USHMM Encyclopedia of Camps and Ghettos*, Vol. 2, 592.
2. Ibid.
3. Karen Wolfers-Rapaport, *Eishet Chayil: A Pictorial View of the Woman of Valor* https://www.chabad.org/theJewishWoman/article_cdo/aid/3270084/jewish/Eishet-Chayil-A-Pictorial-View-of-the-Woman-of-Valor.html (Chabad.org / TheJewishWoman.org, Celebrating Jewish Womanhood, 2016).
4. Ibid.
5. Meir Soloveichik, *The Jewish Mother: A Theology*, originally published in Azure, Spring, 2005.
6. Rabbi Joseph B. Soloveitchik, *Family Redeemed: Essays on Family Relationships* (New York: Toras HaRav Foundation, 2000), 163.

CHAPTER SIX: THE MURDER OF WIELICZKA'S REMAINING JEWS

1. Megargee, *USHMM Encyclopedia of Camps and Ghettos*, Vol. 2, 593.
2. Meiri, *The Jewish Community of Wieliczka*, 41.
3. Spector, *The Encyclopedia of Jewish Life Before and During the Holocaust*, 1442.
4. Ibid.
5. Meiri, *The Jewish Community of Wieliczka*, 42.
6. Ibid., 40.
7. Ibid., 43.
8. Spector, *The Encyclopedia of Jewish Life Before and During the Holocaust*, 1442.
9. Meiri, *The Jewish Community of Wieliczka*, 42.
10. Spector, *The Encyclopedia of Jewish Life Before and During the Holocaust*, 1442.
11. Meiri, *The Jewish Community of Wieliczka*, 43.
12. Megargee, *USHMM Encyclopedia of Camps and Ghettos*, Vol. 2, 489.
13. Ibid., 541.

CHAPTER SEVEN: MY NAME IS STASZEK SURDEL
1. Megargee, *USHMM Encyclopedia of Camps and Ghettos*, vol. 2, 530.

CHAPTER EIGHT: LIBERATION AND THE REALITY OF SURVIVING ALONE
1. Jan T. Gross, *Fear: Anti-Semitism in Poland After Auschwitz* (New York: Random House, 2006), 34–38; 81–117.
2. Ibid., 39–51.

CHAPTER NINE: LEAVING POLAND
[none]

CHAPTER TEN: THE REAL POLAND
1. https://www.yadvashem.org/righteous/statistics.html, no author or year affixed.
2. https://www.yadvashem.org/righteous/stories/poland-historical-background.html, no author or year affixed.
3. Ibid.
4. https://www.bbc.com/news/world-europe-44627129, no author, June 27, 2018.
5. Adam Easton, *Why has Poland backtracked on Holocaust law?* https://www.bbc.com/news/world-europe-44627129, June 27, 2018.
6. Robert Michael, *Holy Hatred: Christianity, Antisemitism, and the Holocaust* (Palgrave MacMillan, 2006), 178.

CHAPTER ELEVEN: THE LAST JEW OF WIELICZKA
1. Primo Levi, *The Drowned and the Saved*, R. Rosenthal (trans.) (New York: Vintage International, 1989), 11–12; paraphrasing Simon Wiesenthal, *The Murderers Are Among Us*, J. Wechsberg (ed.), (Columbus, OH; McGraw-Hill, 1967).

ABOUT THE AUTHOR

JOEL POREMBA is a business attorney with twenty-three years of litigation experience in both state and federal courts. He represents small and medium-sized companies in complex business disputes, and he is graduate of Western State University, College of Law and the University of California, San Diego.

He is the son of Holocaust survivor Nathan Poremba. Stunned after hearing his father give his testimony to the Shoah Foundation in 1998, it took 21 years and an inspiring trip to Israel for Joel to finally watch his father's video testimony and subsequently sit down and to further interview his father about his Holocaust survival.

Joel and Nathan live in Laguna Niguel, California in Orange County.

Learn more at
https://joelporemba.com

CPSIA information can be obtained
at www.ICGtesting.com
Printed in the USA
JSHW040841010522
25453JS00001B/1